AND THE
ANGELS
WERE
SILENT

AND THE ANGELS WERE SILENT

Max Lucado

WORD PUBLISHING
Nelson Word Ltd
Milton Keynes, England

WORD AUSTRALIA
Kilsyth, Victoria, Australia

STRUIK CHRISTIAN BOOKS (PTY) LTD
Maitland, South Africa

**JOINT DISTRIBUTORS SINGAPORE –
ALBY COMMERCIAL ENTERPRISES PTE LTD**
and
CAMPUS CRUSADE

CHRISTIAN MARKETING NEW ZEALAND LTD
Havelock North, New Zealand

JENSCO LTD
Hong Kong

SALVATION BOOK CENTRE
Malaysia

AND THE ANGELS WERE SILENT

Copyright © 1992 by Max Lucado.

First published by Multnomah Press, Portland, Oregon.

First UK edition Nelson Word Ltd., Milton Keynes, England, 1993.

ISBN 0-85009-598-0   (Australia ISBN 1-86258-257-2)

Unless otherwise indicated, all Scripture references are from the Holy Bible: New Century Version, © 1987, 1988, 1991 by Word Publishing, Dallas, Texas 75039. Used by permission.

Scripture references marked NIV are from the Holy Bible: New International Version, © 1973, 1978, 1984 by the International Bible Society. Used by permission of Zondervan Bible Publishers.

Scripture references marked KJV are from the Holy Bible: Authorised King James Version.

Scripture references marked NEB are from The New English Bible, The Delegates of the Oxford University Press and the Syndics of the Cambridge University Press © 1961, 1970. Used by permission.

Scripture references marked RSV are from the Revised Standard Version of the Bible, © 1946, 1952, 1971, 1973, Division of Christian Education, National Council of the Churches in the USA.

Scripture references marked Phillips are from the J. B. Phillips: The New Testament in Modern English, revised edition. J. B. Phillips © 1958, 1960, 1972. Used by permission of Macmillan Publishing Co., Inc.

Study Guide compiled and written by Steve Halliday.

Reproduced, printed and bound in Great Britain for Nelson Word Ltd. by Cox and Wyman Ltd., Reading.

93 94 95 96 / 10 9 8 7 6 5 4 3 2 1

*For my
father- and mother-in-law
Charles and Romadene Preston
for giving me such delight*

Contents

Thursday

Friday

Sunday

Acknowledgments

Here's a salute to some dear people who have made this project possible and pleasant.

To Liz Heaney. You've been more than an editor; you've been a friend.

To John Van Diest. You never forgot the highest aim of Christian publishing—God's Word put into man's heart.

For Brenda Josee. Endless energy and boundless creativity.

For the rest of the Multnomah staff. My hat is off to you guys.

A special word for my secretary Mary Stain. Your retirement and this book deadline came the same month. I was as sorry to see you leave as I was happy to finish the book. Thanks for your tireless efforts.

To Joseph Shulam of Jerusalem. A friend, a brother, and a contagious zealot.

To the Netivyah congregation in Jerusalem. The only unhappy part of our journey to your city was the departure.

To Steve Green. For twenty years of friendship and countless more of partnership.

To the Oak Hills Church. You teach me more than I could ever teach you.

To my daughters Jenna, Andrea, and Sara. If only I could have your innocence and faith.

For my wife Denalyn. When I come home late you don't complain. When I go on the road you don't grumble. When I write in the middle of the night you don't mind. Does every writer have an angel for a wife, or did I get the last one?

And lastly, for you, the reader. If this is your first time with one of my books, I'm honored to be with you. You are entrusting me with your time and your heart. I pledge to be a good steward of both.

If not, if we've spent time together before, it's good to be with you again. My aim in this book is the same as the others: that you will see him and him only.

May I ask something of you? Please remember our work in your prayers. Pray the prayer of Colossians 4:3,4: ". . . that God will give us an opportunity to tell people his message. Pray that we can preach the secret that God has made known about Christ . . . that I can speak in a way that will make it clear, as I should."

A Word Before

It's early in the final week. The props and players for Friday's drama are in position. Six-inch spikes are in the bin. A cross-beam leans against a shed wall. Thorn limbs are wrapped around a trellis awaiting the weaving of a soldier's fingers.

The players are nearing the stage. Pilate is concerned at the number of Passover pilgrims. Annas and Caiaphas are restless over a volatile Nazarene. Judas views his master with furtive eyes. A centurion is available, awaiting the next crucifixions.

Players and props. Only this is no play, it's a divine plan. A plan begun before Adam felt heaven's breath and now all heaven waits and watches. All eyes are on one figure—the Nazarene.

Commonly clad. Uncommonly focused. Leaving Jericho and walking toward Jerusalem. He doesn't chatter. He doesn't pause. He is on a journey. His final journey.

Even the angels are silent. They know this is no ordinary walk. They know this is no ordinary week. For hinged on this week is the door of eternity.

Let's walk with him.

Let's see how Jesus spent his final days.

Let's see what mattered to God.

When a man knows the end is near—only the important surfaces. Impending death distills the vital. The trivial is bypassed. The unnecessary is overlooked. That which is vital remains. So, if you would know Christ, ponder his final days.

He knew the end was near. He knew the finality of Friday. He read the last chapter before it was written and heard the final chorus before it was sung. As a result, the critical was centrifuged from the casual. Distilled truths taught. Deliberate deeds done. Each step calculated. Every act premeditated.

Knowing he had just one week with the disciples, what did Jesus tell them? Knowing it would be his last time in the temple, how did he act? Conscious that the last sand was slipping through the hourglass, what mattered?[1]

Enter the holy week and observe.

Feel his passion. Laughing as children sing. Weeping as Jerusalem ignores. Scorning as priests accuse. Pleading as disciples sleep. Feeling sad as Pilate turns.

Sense his power. Blind eyes . . . seeing. Fruitless tree . . . withering. Money changers . . . scampering. Religious leaders . . . cowering. Tomb . . . opening.

Hear his promise. Death has no power. Failure holds no prisoners. Fear has no control. For God has come, God has come into your world . . . to take you home.

Let's follow Jesus on his final journey. For by observing his, we may learn how to make ours.

Chapter 1

Too Little,
Too Late,
Too Good to Be True

*"Those who have the last place now
will have the first place in the future."*
Matthew 20:16

The only thing slower than Ben's walk was his drawl.

"Waiell, boy," he stretched his words and waited a month between phrases, "looks like it's you and me agin."

Snowy white hair billowed from under his baseball hat. Shoulders stooped. Face leathered from seven decades of West Texas winters.

What I remember most are the eyebrows. Shaggy hedges on the crest of his forehead. Caterpillars that shifted with his eyes.

He looked at the ground a lot when he talked. He was already short. This only made him seem shorter. When he wanted to make a point he would lift his eyes and flash a glance at you through his bushy brows. He fired this look at anyone who questioned his ability to work in the oil field. But most everybody did anyway.

I owe my acquaintance with Ben to my dad who was convinced school holidays were made for boys to earn money. Like it or not, be it Christmas, summer, or Thanksgiving, he'd wake my brother and me before the sun was up and drop us off at one of the local roustabout companies to see if we could hire on for the day.

Work in the oil field has about as many ups and downs as a drilling rig, so unless you were a company man or had your own crew, there was no guarantee of work. Roustabouts began showing up long before the boss did. Didn't make any difference who got there first, though, all that mattered was the strength of your back and the experience under your belt.

That's where Ben and I came up short. I had the good back, but not the experience; Ben had the calloused hands, but not the strength. So unless there was an especially big job that justified quantity over quality, Ben and I usually were passed over.

The elements of the morning became so predictable that now, twenty years later, I can still taste and feel them.

I can feel the bitter wind as it stung my ears in the early morning blackness. I can feel the frozen handle on the heavy metal door that opened into the work shed. I can hear Ben's gruff voice coming from the stove he had already lit and sat beside: "Shut the door, boy. It's gonna git colder 'fore it gets warmer."

I'd follow the golden light from the stove through the dark shed and turn my back to the fire and look at Ben. He'd be smoking, sitting on a fifty-gallon drum. His work boots would be a foot off the ground and the collar of his coat turned up around his neck.

"Shor do need the work, today, boy. Shor do need the work."

Other workers would begin to trickle in. Each one's arrival lessened any chance Ben and I had of going out. Soon the air would cloud with smoke and bad jokes and complaints about having to work in weather too cold for jack rabbits.

Ben never said much.

After a while the foreman would come in. Sounds funny, but I used to get a bit nervous as the boss walked into the shed to read the list. With the eloquence of a drill sergeant he would bark out what he needed and who he wanted. "Need six hands to clean a battery today," or, "Putting in a new line in the south field, gonna need eight."

Then he would announce his list, "Buck, Tom, Happy, and Jack—come with me."

There was a certain honor about being chosen . . . something special about being singled out, even if it was to dig ditches. But just as there was an honor with being chosen, there was a certain shame about being left behind. Again.

The only rung lower on the oil field caste system than the roustabout was the unemployment line. If you couldn't weld, then you would roughneck. If you couldn't roughneck, then you'd service wells. If you couldn't service wells, then you'd roustabout. But if you couldn't roustabout . . .

More times than not Ben and I couldn't roustabout. Those of us who went unchosen would hang around the stove for a few minutes and make excuses about how we really didn't want to go out anyway. Soon everyone would meander out leaving Ben and me alone in the work shed. We had no better place to go. Besides, you never knew when another job might surface. So we waited.

That's when Ben would talk. Weaving fact with fiction he would spin stories of wildcatting with divining rods and mules. The dawn would become day as the two of us sat on tire rims or paint buckets and walked the dusty roads of Ben's memory.

We were quite a pair. In many ways we were opposites: me barely fifteen years into the world, Ben into his seventieth winter. Me—crisp and convinced that the best was yet to come. Ben—weathered and crusty, living off of yesterday's accolades.

But we came to be friends. For in the oil field we were common cast outs. Fellow failures. The "too little, too lates."

Do you know what I'm talking about? Are you one too?

Sherri is. After three children and twelve years of marriage, her husband found a wife a bit younger. A newer model. Sherri got left behind.

Mr. Robinson is. Three decades with the same company had him one office from the top. When the executive retired, he knew it was only a matter of time. The board, however, had different ideas. They wanted youth. The one thing Robinson didn't have. He got picked over.

Manuel can tell you. At least he would if he could. It's tough being one of nine children in a fatherless home in the Rio Grande Valley. For Manuel it's even harder. He's a deaf mute. Even if there were a school for the deaf he could attend, he has no money.

"A lost ball in tall grass."

"A day late and a dollar short."

"Small guy in a tall world."

"One brick short of a load."

You pick the phrase—the result is still the same. Get told enough times that only the rotten fruit gets left in the bin, and you begin to believe it. You begin to believe you are "too little, too late."

If that describes you, then you are holding the right book at the right time. You see, God has a peculiar passion for the forgotten. Have you noticed?

See his hand on the festered skin of the leper?

See the face of the prostitute cupped in his hands?

Notice how he responds to the touch of the woman with the hemorrhage?

See him with his arm around little Zacchaeus?

Over and over again God wants us to get the message: He has a peculiar passion for the forgotten. What society puts out, God puts in. What the world writes off, God picks up. That must be why Jesus told the story of the chosen workers. It's the first story of his final week. It's the last story he will tell before entering Jerusalem. Once inside the city walls Jesus becomes a marked man. The hourglass will be turned and the final countdown and chaos will begin.

But it's not Jerusalem. And he's not addressing his enemies. It's the Jericho countryside and he's with friends. And for them he weaves this parable of grace.

A certain landowner needs workers. At 6:00 A.M. he picks his crew, they agree on a wage, and he puts them to work. At 9:00 he is back at the unemployment agency and picks a few more. At noon he is back and at 3:00 in the afternoon he is back and at 5:00, you guessed it. He's back again.

Now, the punchline of the story is the anger the twelve-hour laborers felt when the other guys got the same wage. That's a great message, but we'll save it for another book.

I want to hone in on an often forgotten scene in the story: the choosing. Can you see it? It happened at 9:00. It happened at noon. It happened at 3:00. But most passionately, it happened at 5:00.

Five in the afternoon. Tell me. What is a worker still doing in the yard at 5:00 in the afternoon? The best have long since gone. The mediocre workers went at lunch. The last string went at 3:00. What kind of worker is left at 5:00 P.M.?

All day they get passed by. They are unskilled. Untrained. Uneducated. They are hanging with one hand from the bottom of the ladder. They are absolutely dependent upon a merciful boss giving them a chance they don't deserve.

So, by the way, were we. Lest we get a bit cocky, we might take Paul's advice and look at what we were when God called us.[1] Do you remember?

Some of us were polished and sharp but papier-mâché thin. Others of us didn't even try to hide our despair. We drank it. We smelled it. We shot it. We sold it. Life was a passion-pursuit. We were on a treasure hunt for an empty chest in a dead-end canyon.

Do you remember how you felt? Do you remember the perspiration on your forehead and the crack in your soul? Do you remember how you tried to hide the loneliness until it got bigger than you and then you just tried to survive?

Hold that picture for a moment. Now answer this. Why did he choose you? Why did he choose me? Honestly. Why? What do we have that he needs?

Intellect? Do we honestly think for one minute that we have— or ever will have—a thought he hasn't had?

Willpower? I can respect that. Some of us are stubborn enough to walk on water if we felt called to do so . . . but to think God's kingdom would have done a belly-up without our determination?

How about money? We came into the kingdom with a nice little nest egg. Perhaps that's why we were chosen. Perhaps the creator of heaven and earth could use a little of our cash. Maybe the owner of every breath and every person and the author of history was getting low on capital and he saw us and our black ink and . . .

Get the point?

We were chosen for the same reason the five o'clock workers were. You and me? We are the five o'clock workers.

That's us leaning against the orchard fence sucking cigarettes we can't afford and betting beers we'll never buy on a game of penny-toss. Migrant workers with no jobs and no futures. The tattoo on your arm reads "Betty." The one on my biceps is nameless but her hips bounce when I flex. We should have given up and gone home after the lunch whistle but home is a one-bedroom motel with a wife whose first question will be, "Did you get on or not?"

So we wait. The too little, too lates.

And Jesus? Well, Jesus is the guy in the black pickup who owns the hillside acreage. He's the fellow who noticed us as he drove by leaving us in his dust. He's the one who stopped the truck, put it in reverse, and backed up to where we were standing.

He's the one you'll tell your wife about tonight as you walk to the grocery with a jingle in your pocket. "I'd never seen this guy before. He just stopped, rolled down his window, and asked us if we wanted to work. It was already near quitting time, but he said he had some work that wouldn't wait. I swear, Martha, I only worked one hour and he paid me for the full day."

"No, I don't know his name."

"Of course, I'm gonna find out. Too good to be true, that guy."

Why did he pick you? He wanted to. After all, you are his. He made you. He brought you home. He owns you. And once upon a time, he tapped you on the shoulder and reminded you of that fact.

No matter how long you'd waited or how much time you'd wasted, you are his and he has a place for you.

"You guys still need some work?"

Ben jumped down from the barrel and answered for both of us. "Yes sir."

"Grab your hats and lunches and get in the truck."

We didn't have to be told twice. I'd already eaten my lunch but I grabbed the pail anyway. We jumped in the back of the flatbed and leaned against the cab. Old Ben put a smoke in his mouth and cupped his hand around the match to protect it from the wind. As the truck began to rumble, he spoke. Though it's been twenty years I still can see his eyes sparkle through the furry brows.

"Shor feels good to be chosen, don't it, boy?"

Sure does, Ben. It sure does.

Chapter 2

From Jericho to Jerusalem

"They will give the Son of Man to the non-Jewish people to laugh at him and beat him with whips and crucify him. But on the third day, he will be raised to life again."
Matthew 20:19

As far as Father Alexander Borisov knew, he would never come back alive. The black Russian night held no assurance of safety. He hoped the police would be intimidated by his flowing black and gold vestments, but there was no guarantee.

Moscow was under siege. The hibernating bear had awakened from her winter sleep and was hungry. Precedent promised to oppress the people once more.

But Borisov dared to defy precedence. On August 20, 1991, he and a few members of the one-year-old Bible Society of the Soviet Union stalked tanks while carrying bundles of New Testaments. If crews declined face-to-face talks, the priest climbed on board the tanks and pitched the Bibles through the hatches.

"In my heart, I believed that soldiers with New Testaments in their pockets would not shoot their brothers and sisters," he later said.

Insightful. Better to go to battle with God's Word in your heart than mighty weapons in your hand.

But Moscow is far from the first demonstration of that. For the most poignant portrayal of someone marching to battle with God's truth, don't go to Russia. Don't read the Associated Press. Don't watch the six o'clock news. Go instead to Scripture and highlight a paragraph you never may have noticed.

It's easy to miss. Only three verses. Only eighty-five words. There is nothing to set them apart as unique. No dramatic lead. No bold letters. No arresting titles. So matter-of-fact is the statement that the casual reader might dismiss it as a transition. But to do so is to leave the quarry without seeing the jewel.

Only one event. It hasn't the flair of a resurrection of Lazarus. Certainly not the scale of the five thousand fed. Gone is the magic of the manger. Missing is the drama of the stilled storm. It's a quiet moment in Scripture. But don't be fooled. For at this moment no angel dared sing.

Only one road. Just fourteen miles. A half-day's journey through a treacherous canyon. But it's not the road that should capture our attention. Dusty roads were common back then. No, it's not the road, it's where it goes—and it's the man who walks it.

He is at the front of his band. Nowhere else do we find Jesus at the head. Not when he descended the mountain after the Sermon on the Mount. Not after he left Capernaum. Not as he entered the village of Nain. He usually chose to be surrounded by people rather than out in front of them.

Not this time. Mark tells us that Jesus was out in front.[1] Only one man. A young soldier marching into battle.

If you want to know someone's heart, observe that person's final journey.

The story of young Matthew Huffman came across my desk the week I was writing this chapter. He was the six-year-old son of missionaries in Salvador, Brazil. One morning he began to complain of fever. As his temperature went up, he began losing his eyesight. His mother and father put him in the car and raced him to the hospital.

As they were driving and he was lying on his mother's lap, he did something his parents will never forget. He extended his hand in the air. His mother took it and he pulled it away. He extended it again. She again took it and he, again, pulled it back and reached into the air. Confused, the mother asked her son, "What are you reaching for, Matthew?"

"I'm reaching for Jesus' hand," he answered. And with those words he closed his eyes and slid into a coma from which he never would awaken. He died two days later, a victim of bacterial meningitis.

Of all the things he didn't learn in his short life, he'd learned the most important: who to reach for in the hour of death.

You can tell a lot about a person by the way he dies. Consider the example of Jim Bonham.

Of all the heroes of the Alamo, none is better known than James Bonham, the fiery young lawyer from South Carolina. He had been in Texas for only three months, but his yearning for freedom left him no choice but to march alongside these Texans in their battle for liberty. He volunteered for service at the Alamo, a small mission near the Guadalupe River. As the Mexican army filled the horizon and the tiny bastion poised for battle, Bonham broke through the enemy cordon and galloped eastward to Goliad for help.

In his book *Texas*, James Michener imagines what the soldier's appeal must have been: "Outside were a hundred and fifty men. Santa Anna has nearly two thousand already, with more on the way. . . . What we need is for every fighting man in Texas to rush to the Alamo. Strengthen our perimeters! Give us help! Start to march now!"

No commitment was given. The only assurance Colonel Fannin gave Bonham was that he would think it over. The young Carolinian knew what that meant and he masked his anger and spurred his horse on to Victoria.

Michener imagines a conversation between Bonham and a young boy.

"Where are you going next?" the boy asks.

"To the Alamo," Bonham responds without hesitation.

"Will you go back alone?"

"I came alone."

As Bonham disappears, the boy asks his father, "If things are so bad, why does he go back in?"

To which the father responds, "I doubt if he considered any other possibility."[2]

We don't know if those words were said, but we know the trip was made. Bonham rode to battle certain it would be his last.

So did Jesus. With the final mission before him, he stopped his disciples and told them for the third time of his conclusive encounter with the enemy. "We are going to Jerusalem. The Son of Man will be turned over to the leading priests and the teachers of the law, and they will say that he must die. They will give the Son of Man to the non-Jewish people to laugh at him and beat him with whips and crucify him. But on the third day he will be raised to life again."[3]

Note his detailed knowledge of the event. He tells who—"the leading priests and teachers of the law." He tells what—"they will give the Son of Man to the non-Jewish people to laugh at him and beat him with whips and crucify him." He tells when—"but on the third day he will be raised to life again."

Forget any suggestion that Jesus was trapped. Erase any theory that Jesus made a miscalculation. Ignore any speculation that the cross was a last-ditch attempt to salvage a dying mission.

For if these words tell us anything, they tell us that Jesus died . . . on purpose. No surprise. No hesitation. No faltering.

You can tell a lot about a person by the way he dies. And the way Jesus marched to his death leaves no doubt: he had come to earth for this moment. Read the words of Peter. "Jesus was given to you, and with the help of those who don't know the law, you put him to death by nailing him to a cross. But this was God's plan which he had made long ago; he knew all this would happen."[4]

No, the journey to Jerusalem didn't begin in Jericho. It didn't begin in Galilee. It didn't begin in Nazareth. It didn't even begin in Bethlehem.

The journey to the cross began long before. As the echo of the crunching of the fruit was still sounding in the garden, Jesus was leaving for Calvary.

And just as Father Alexander Borisov walked into battle with the Word of God in his hand, Jesus stepped toward Jerusalem with the promise of God in his heart. The divinity of Christ assured the humanity of Christ, and Jesus spoke loud enough for the pits of hell to vibrate: "But on the third day he will be raised to life again."

Is there a Jerusalem on your horizon? Are you a brief journey away from painful encounters? Are you only steps away from the walls of your own heartache?

Learn a lesson from your master. Don't march into battle with the enemy without first claiming the courage from God's promises. May I give you a few examples?

When you are confused: " 'I know what I am planning for you,' says the LORD. 'I have good plans for you, not plans to hurt you.' "[5]

If you feel weighted by yesterday's failures: "So now, those who are in Christ Jesus are not judged guilty."[6]

On those nights when you wonder where God is: "I am the Holy One, and I am among you."[7]

If you think you can fall beyond God's love: "Understand the greatness of Christ's love—how wide and how long and how high and how deep that love is. Christ's love is greater than anyone can ever know."[8]

Next time you find yourself on a Jericho road marching toward Jerusalem, put the promises of God on your lips. When the blackness of oppression settles on your city, remember the convictions of Father Borisov.

By the way, Bible Society workers in Moscow will long remember the story of one soldier who did just that. In the early hours of August 20 they offered him a colorful children's Bible since they were out of smaller New Testaments. The soldier realized he would need to hide it from his superiors if he were to take it home. But his uniform had only one pocket large enough.

The soldier hesitated, then emptied his ammunition pocket. He went on to the barricade with a Bible instead of bullets.

'Tis wise to march into Jerusalem with the promise of God in your heart. It was for Alexander Borisov. It was for Matthew Huffman. And it is for you.

Chapter 3

The Sacrificial General

"In the same way, the Son of Man did not come to be served. He came to serve others and to give his life as a ransom for many people."
Matthew 20:28

The decision had been made. The troops had been deployed and the battleships were on their way. Nearly three million soldiers were preparing to slam against Hitler's Atlantic wall in France. D-Day was set in motion. Responsibility for the invasion fell squarely on the four-starred shoulders of General Dwight D. Eisenhower.

The general spent the night before the attack with the men of the 101st Airborne. They called themselves The Screaming Eagles. As his men prepared their planes and checked their equipment, Ike went from soldier to soldier offering words of encouragement. Many of the flyers were young enough to be his sons. He treated them like they were. A correspondent wrote that as Eisenhower watched the C-47s take off and disappear into the darkness, his hands were sunk deeply into his pockets and his eyes were full of tears.

The general then went to his quarters and sat at his desk. He took a pen and paper and wrote a message—a message which would be delivered to the White House in the event of a defeat.

It was as brief as it was courageous. "Our landings . . . have failed . . . the troops, the Air, and the Navy did all that bravery and devotion to duty could do. If any blame or fault attaches itself to the attempt it was mine alone."[1]

It could be argued that the greatest act of courage that day was not in a cockpit or foxhole, but at a desk when the one at the top took responsibility for the ones below. When the one in charge took the blame—even before the blame needed to be taken.

Rare leader, this general. Unusual, this display of courage. He modeled a quality seldom seen in our society of lawsuits, dismissals, and divorces. Most of us are willing to take credit for the good we do. Some are willing to take the rap for the bad we do. But few will assume responsibilities for the mistakes of others. Still fewer will shoulder the blame for mistakes yet uncommitted.

Eisenhower did. As a result, he became a hero.

Jesus did. As a result, he's our Savior.

Before the war began, he forgave. Before a mistake could be made, forgiveness was offered. Before blame could be given, grace was provided.

The one at the top took responsibility for the ones at the bottom. Read how Jesus describes what he came to do.

"The Son of Man did not come to be served. He came to serve others and to give his life as a ransom for many people."[2]

The phrase "Son of Man" conjured the same images for the Jew of Christ's era that the title "general" creates for you and me. It was a statement of authority and power.

Consider all the titles Jesus could have used to define himself on earth: King of kings, the great I AM, the Beginning and the End, the Lord of All, Jehovah, High and Holy. All of these and a dozen others would have been appropriate.

But Jesus didn't use them.

Instead, he called himself the Son of Man. This title appears eighty-two times in the New Testament. Eighty-one of which are in the Gospels. Eighty of which are directly from the lips of Jesus.

To understand Jesus we need to understand what this title means. If Jesus thought it important enough to use over eighty times, it is certainly important enough for us to explore.

Few would argue that the title is rooted in Daniel 7, a text which is just one frame of a cinematographic masterpiece. The seer is afforded a seat in a theater that features a peek at the future powers of the earth. The empires are portrayed as beasts: rabid, hungry, and vicious. The lion with the eagle's wings[3] stands for Babylonia, and the bear with three ribs in its mouth[4] represents Medo Persia. Alexander the Great is symbolized by a leopard with four wings and four heads,[5] and a fourth beast with iron teeth represents Rome.[6]

But as the scenes unfold the empires fade. One by one the world powers tumble. At the end the conquering God, the Ancient of Days, receives into his presence the Son of Man. To him is entrusted authority, glory, and sovereign power.[7] Picture him blazing white. Atop a gallant steed. A sword in his hand.

To the Jew the Son of Man was a symbol of triumph. The conqueror. The equalizer. The score-settler. The big brother. The intimidator. The Starship *Enterprise*. The right arm of the High and Holy. The king who roared down from the heavens in a fiery chariot of vengeance and anger toward those who have oppressed God's holy people.[8]

The Son of Man was the four-starred general who called his army to invade and led his troops to victory.

For that reason when Jesus spoke of the Son of Man in terms of power, the people cheered.

When he spoke of a new world where the Son of Man would sit on his glorious throne[9], the people understood.

When he spoke of the Son of Man who would come on the clouds of heaven with great power and authority[10], the people could envision the scene.

When he spoke of the Son of Man seated at the right hand of power[11], everyone could imagine the picture.

But when he said the Son of Man would suffer . . . the people stood silent. This didn't fit the image . . . it's not what they expected.

Put yourself in their place. You've been oppressed by the Roman government for years. Since your youth you've been taught that the Son of Man would deliver you. Now he's here. Jesus calls himself the Son of Man. He proves he is the Son of Man. He can raise the dead and still a storm. The crowds of followers are growing. You are excited. Finally, the children of Abraham will be set free.

But what's this he's saying? "The Son of Man did not come to be served. He came to serve others." Earlier he'd told them, "The Son of Man will be handed over to people, and they will kill him. After three days, he will rise from the dead."[12]

Wait a minute! That's an impossible, incredible, intolerable contradiction of terms. No wonder "the followers did not understand what Jesus meant, and they were afraid to ask him."[13] The king who came to serve? The Son of Man being betrayed? The Conqueror—killed? The Ambassador of the Ancient of Days— mocked? Spit upon?

But such is the irony of Jesus wearing the title "the Son of Man." It is also the irony of the cross. Calvary is a hybrid of God's lofty status and his deep devotion. The thunderclap which echoed when God's sovereignty collided with his love. The marriage of heaven's kingship and heaven's compassion.[14] The very instrument of the cross is symbolic, the vertical beam of holiness intersecting with the horizontal bar of love.

Jesus wears a sovereign crown but bears a father's heart.

He is a general who takes responsibility for his soldiers' mistakes.

But Jesus didn't write a note, he paid the price. He didn't just assume the blame, he seized the sin. He became the ransom. He is the General who dies in the place of the private, the King who suffers for the peasant, the Master who sacrifices himself for the servant.

As a young boy, I read a Russian fable about a master and a servant who went on a journey to a city. Many of the details I've forgotten but the ending I remember. Before the two men could reach the destination they were caught in a blinding blizzard. They lost their direction and were unable to reach the city before nightfall.

The next morning concerned friends went searching for the two men. They finally found the master, frozen to death, face down in the snow. When they lifted him they found the servant—cold but alive. He survived and told how the master had voluntarily placed himself on top of the servant so the servant could live.

I hadn't thought of that story in years. But when I read what Christ said he would do for us, the story surfaced—for Jesus is the Master who died for the servants.

He is the general who made provision for his soldiers' mistakes.

He is the Son of Man who came to serve and to give his life as a ransom . . . for you.

Chapter 4

Ugly Religion

"Jesus felt sorry for the blind men and touched their eyes, and at once they could see."
Matthew 20:34

It happens in business when you make products you don't market.

It happens in government when you keep departments you don't need.

It happens in medicine when your research never leaves the lab.

It happens in education when your goal is grades, not learning.

And it happened on the road to Jerusalem when Jesus' disciples wouldn't let the blind men come to Christ.

"When Jesus and his followers were leaving Jericho, a great many people followed him. Two blind men sitting by the road heard that Jesus was going by, so they shouted, 'Lord, Son of David, have mercy on us!' "[1]

The people warned the blind men to be quiet, but they called out even louder, "Lord, Son of David, have mercy on us!"

Jesus stopped and said to the blind men, "What do you want me to do for you?"

They answered, "Lord, we want to see."

Jesus "touched their eyes, and at once they could see. Then they followed Jesus."[2]

Matthew doesn't tell us why the people refused to let the blind men get close to Jesus—but it's easy to figure it out. They want to protect him. He's on a mission, a critical mission. The future of Israel is at stake. He is an important man with a crucial task. He hasn't time for indigents on the side of the road.

Besides, look at them. Dirty. Loud. Obnoxious. Embarrassing. Don't they have any sense of propriety? Don't they have any dignity? These things must be handled in the proper procedure. First talk to Nathaniel who talks to John who talks to Peter who then decides if the matter is worth troubling the Master or not.

But despite their sincerity, the disciples were wrong.

And so, by the way, are we when we think God is too busy for little people or too formal for poor protocol. When people are refused access to Christ by those closest to him, the result is empty, hollow religion. Ugly religion.

A striking parallel to this occurred in a San Antonio hospital.

Paul Loetz took a bad fall that left him with a punctured lung, broken ribs, and internal bruising. Lying in an emergency room, barely conscious, he probably thought things couldn't get much worse.

They did.

As he looked up from his hospital bed, the two doctors responsible for his care began arguing over who would get to put a tube into his crushed chest. The argument became a shoving match and one doctor threatened to have the other removed by security police.

"Please, somebody save my life," Loetz pleaded as doctors fought over him.[3]

The two doctors were arguing over procedure. While they were debating two other physicians assumed responsibility for the patient and saved his life.

Hard to believe isn't it? Needs ignored while opinions are disputed? Yet it happens—even in the church. I got a call this week from a man who listens to my radio program. He grew up in a non-Christian home. He works, however, with two Christians of two denominations. I thought it strange he called me when he had Christians as co-workers. Then he told me, "One says this and one says that. All I want to do is find Jesus."

It happens today.

It happens when a church spends more time discussing the style of its sanctuary than it does the needs of the hungry. It happens when the brightest minds of the church occupy themselves with dull controversies rather than majestic truths. It happens when a church is known more for its stance on an issue than its reliance upon God.

It happens today. And it happened then.

You see, in the eyes of those closest to Jesus, these blind men had no right to interfere with the Master. After all, he is on his way to Jerusalem. The Son of Man is going to establish the kingdom. He has no time to hear the needs of some blind beggars on the side of the road.

So, the people warned the blind men to be quiet.

They are a nuisance, these beggars. Look at the way they are dressed. Look at the way they act. Look at the way they cry for help. Jesus has more important things to do than to be bothered by such insignificant people.

Christ thought otherwise. Jesus "felt sorry for the blind men and touched their eyes, and at once they could see."

Jesus hears them in spite of the clamor. And of all the people, it is the blind who really see Jesus.

Something told these two beggars that God is more concerned with the right heart than he is the right clothes or procedure. Somehow they knew that what they lacked in method could be made up for in motive, so they called out at the top of their lungs. And they were heard.

God always hears those who seek him. May I give another case in point? Go back in history a few centuries.

Hezekiah, king of Israel, stirrer of religious revival in the land, calls upon the people to abandon false Gods and return to the true God. He calls upon the people to come to Jerusalem to celebrate the Passover. But there are two problems.

One, it has been so long since the people partook of the Passover that no one is ceremonially clean. No one is prepared to partake. Even the priests have been worshiping idols and have failed to observe the necessary rituals for purity.

Two, God had commanded that the Passover be celebrated on the fourteenth day of the first month. By the time Hezekiah can assemble the people, it is the second month.

So the Passover was kept a month late by impure participants.

Hezekiah prayed for them: " 'LORD, you are good. . . . Please forgive all those who try to obey you even if they did not make themselves clean as the rules of the Temple command.'"[4]

Do you see the dilemma?

What does God do when the motive is pure but the method is poor?

"The LORD listened to Hezekiah's prayer, and he healed the people."[5]

The right heart with the wrong ritual is better than the wrong heart with the right ritual.

Some time ago I was in Atlanta, Georgia, at a conference. I called home and talked to Denalyn and the girls. Jenna was about five at the time and said she had a special treat for me. She took the phone over to the piano and began to play an original composition.

From a musical standpoint, everything was wrong with the song. She pounded more than she played. There was more random than rhythm in the piece. The lyrics didn't rhyme. The syntax was sinful. Technically the song was a failure.

But to me, the song was a masterpiece. Why? Because she wrote it for me.

You are a great daddy.
I miss you very much.
When you're away I'm very sad and I cry.
Please come home very soon.

What dad wouldn't like that? What father wouldn't bask in the praise of even an off-key adulation?

Some of you are scowling. "Wait a minute, Max. Are you saying that the method we use to approach God is immaterial? Are you saying that the only thing that matters is why we go to God and that how we approach him is relative?"

No, that's not what I'm saying (but I do appreciate the question). Ideally, we approach God with the right motive and the right method. And sometimes we do. Sometimes the words of our prayer are as beautiful as the motive behind the prayer. Sometimes the way we sing is as strong as the reason we sing.

Sometimes our worship is as attractive as it is sincere.

But many times it isn't. Many times our words falter. Many times our music suffers. Many times our worship is less than what we want it to be. Many times our appeals for God's presence are about as attractive as those of the blind men on the side of the road.

"Lord, help."

And sometimes, even today, sincere disciples will tell us to be quiet until we can do it right.

Jesus didn't tell the blind men to be quiet. God didn't tell Hezekiah to shut down the celebration. I didn't tell Jenna to practice a bit and call me again after she had improved.

The blind men, Hezekiah, and Jenna all did the best they could with what they had—and that was enough.

"You will search for me," God declared. "And when you search for me with all your heart, you will find me! I will let you find me."[6]

What a promise! And with the blind beggars, he proved it.

The last scene in the story is worth capturing. The two scraggly dressed, smelly but bright-eyed beggars are walking—no, skipping—behind Jesus on the road to Jerusalem. Pointing at flowers they'd always smelled but never seen. Looking into the sun they'd always felt but never witnessed. Ironic. Of all the people on the road that day, they turned out to be the ones with the clearest vision—even before they could see.

Chapter 5

Don't Just Do Something, Stand There

"Work and get everything done during six days each week, but the seventh day is a day of rest to honor the LORD your God."
Exodus 20:9-10

I took my daughter Andrea on a walk some time ago. She was four and curious, so we went to explore our neighborhood. "Let's cover some new territory," I suggested. Off we went, striding confidently out of the safe harbor of our cul-de-sac and stepping into unknown regions.

Captain Kirk would have been proud.

The area was brand new to her. We walked down streets she'd never seen and petted dogs she'd never touched. Virgin territory. Wilderness wanderings. The yards were different. The kids looked older. The houses looked bigger.

I thought all the change might trouble her. I thought the new sights and sounds might generate anxiety.

"Are you okay?" I asked.

"Sure."

"Do you know where we are?"

"No."

"Do you know how to get home?"

"No."

"And you aren't worried?"

Without slowing her pace she reached up and took my hand and said, "I don't have to know how to get home. You already do."

God once did with his children what I did with Andrea. He led them into a strange land. He marched them through a sea and guided them into unexplored territory.

They didn't know where they were. The desert was strange. The sounds were new and the scenery unfamiliar. But one thing was different: they weren't as trusting as Andrea.

"Take us back to Egypt," they demanded.

But the Father wanted his children to trust him. The Father wanted his children to take his hand and relax. The Father wanted his children to quit worrying about *how* and be content with *who*.

He liberated them from slavery and created a path through the sea. He gave them a cloud to follow in the day and a fire to see at night. And he gave them food. He met their most basic need: he filled their bellies.

Twice a day the manna came. Twice a day the quails appeared. "Trust me. Trust me and I will give you what you need." The people were told to take just enough for one day. Their needs would be met, one day at a time. Despite God's faithfulness in keeping his promise, the people had a hard time believing their provision was the work of God. It went against their logic to see food and not hoard it.

"What if he forgets tomorrow? What if he doesn't come back?" So they would take more than one day's share of food. Overnight the food would spoil.

"Just take enough for today," was God's message. "Let me worry about tomorrow."

The Father wanted the people to trust him.

On Friday they were told to collect a two day's supply of food, for the next day was the Sabbath—the day God set aside for humankind to meet their Creator. On the Sabbath the food collected from the day before would not spoil.

But on the Sabbath the people had a hard time sitting still. It went against common sense to pause and listen when they could get up and work. So, in spite of God's command they went out and gathered food.

(Funny how it is the weary who are most reluctant to rest.)

Note God's wisdom. We need one day in which work comes to a screeching halt. We need one twenty-four hour period in which the wheels stop grinding and the motor stops turning. We need to stop.

The Sabbath is the day that God's children in a foreign land squeeze their Father's hand and say, "I don't know where I am. I don't know how I'll get home. But you do and that's enough."

A couple of weeks ago Andrea and I went on another adventure—this time on bicycles. She had just learned to keep her balance on a two-wheeler and was ready to leave the safety of the front street and try the hill behind our house. She'd never ridden down a hill before.

We sat atop the descent and looked down it. To her it was Everest. "You sure you want to try?" I asked.

"I think so," she gulped.

"Just put on your brakes when you want to stop. Don't forget your brakes."

"Okay."

I rode to the midway point and waited. Down she came. The bike began to pick up speed. The handlebars began to shake. Her eyes got big. Her pedals moved in a blur. As she raced past she screamed, "I can't remember how to stop pedaling!"

She crashed into the curb.

If you don't know how to stop, the result can be painful. True on bikes. True in life.

Do you remember how to stop?

Ever feel like you're racing downhill on a runaway bike and you don't remember how to brake? Ever feel the wheels of your life racing faster and faster as you speed past the people you love? Could you use a reminder on how to slow it all down?

If so read what Jesus did during the last Sabbath of his life. Start in the Gospel of Matthew. Didn't find anything? Try Mark. Read what Mark recorded about the way Jesus spent the Sabbath. Nothing there either? Strange. What about Luke? What does Luke say? Not a reference to the day? Not a word about it? Well, try John. Surely John mentions the Sabbath. He doesn't? No reference? Hmmmm. Looks like Jesus was quiet that day.

"Wait a minute. That's it?" That's it.

"You mean with one week left to live, Jesus observed the Sabbath?" As far as we can tell.

"You mean with all those apostles to train and people to teach, he took a day to rest and worship?" Apparently so.

"You're telling me that Jesus thought worship was more important than work?" That's exactly what I'm telling you.

For such is the purpose of the Sabbath. And such was the practice of Jesus. "On the Sabbath day he went to the synagogue, *as he always did*, and stood up to read."[1] Should we do any less?

If Jesus found time in the midst of a racing agenda to stop the rush and sit in the silence, do you think we could, too?

Ahh, I know what you're thinking. I can see it in your face. There you are. Looking at me from my monitor with dubious eyes and furrowed brows. "But, Max, Sunday is the only day I have to get caught up at the office." Or, "Good idea, Max, but have you heard our preacher? He provides the rest all right—I fall asleep! But the worship?" Or, "That's easy for you to say, Max. You're a preacher. If you were a housewife like me and had four kids like mine . . ." It's not easy to slow down.

It's almost as if activity is a sign of maturity. After all, isn't there a beatitude which reads, "Blessed are the busy?" No, there isn't. But there is a verse which summarizes many lives: "Man is a mere phantom as he goes to and fro: He bustles about, but only in vain; he heaps up wealth, not knowing who will get it."[2]

Does that sound like your life? Are you so seldom in one place that your friends regard you as a phantom? Are you so constantly on the move that your family is beginning to question your existence? Do you take pride in your frenzy at the expense of your faith?

Are Andrea's words yours? "I don't remember how to stop." If so, you are headed for a crash.

Slow down. If God commanded it, you need it. If Jesus modeled it, you need it. God still provides the manna. Trust him. Take a day to say no to work and yes to worship.

One final thought.

One of the reference points of London is the Charing Cross. It is near the geographical center of the city and serves as a navigational tool for those confused by the streets.

A little girl was lost in the great city. A policeman found her. Between sobs and tears, she explained she didn't know her way home. He asked her if she knew her address. She didn't. He asked her phone number; she didn't know that either. But when he asked her what she knew, suddenly her face lit up.

"I know the Cross," she said, "show me the Cross and I can find my way home from there."

So can you. Keep a clear vision of the cross on your horizon and you can find your way home. Such is the purpose of your day of rest: to relax your body, but more importantly to restore your vision. A day in which you get your bearings so you can find your way home.

Do yourself a favor. Reach up and take your father's hand and say what Andrea said to me, "I'm not sure where I am. I'm not sure which is the road home. But you do and that's enough."

Chapter 6

Risky Love

"Mary brought in a pint of very expensive perfume made from pure nard. She poured the perfume on Jesus' feet, and then she wiped his feet with her hair. And the sweet smell from the perfume filled the whole house."

John 12:3

Artful Eddie lacked nothing.

He was the slickest of the slick lawyers. He was one of the roars of the Roaring Twenties. A crony of Al Capone, he ran the gangster's dog tracks. He mastered the simple technique of fixing the race by overfeeding seven dogs and betting on the eighth.

Wealth. Status. Style. Artful Eddie lacked nothing.

Then why did he turn himself in? Why did he offer to squeal on Capone? What was his motive? Didn't Eddie know the sure-fire consequences of ratting on the mob?

He knew, but he'd made up his mind.

What did he have to gain? What could society give him that he didn't have? He had money, power, prestige. What was the hitch?

Eddie revealed the hitch. His son. Eddie had spent his life with the despicable. He had smelled the stench of the underground long enough. For his son, he wanted more. He wanted to give his son a name. And to give his son a name, he would have to clear his own.

Eddie was willing to take a risk so that his son could have a clean slate. Artful Eddie never saw his dream come true. After Eddie squealed, the mob remembered. Two shotgun blasts silenced him forever.

Was it worth it?

For the son it was. Artful Eddie's boy lived up to the sacrifice. His is one of the best-known names in the world.

But, before we talk about the son let's talk about the principle: risky love. Love that takes a chance. Love that goes out on a limb. Love that makes a statement and leaves a legacy. Sacrificial love.

Love which is unexpected, surprising, and stirring. Acts of love which steal the heart and leave impressions on the soul. Acts of love which are never forgotten.

Such an act of love was seen in the last week of the life of Jesus. A demonstration of devotion which the world will never forget. An act of extravagant tenderness in which Jesus wasn't the giver, he was the receiver.

A cluster of friends encircle Jesus. They are at the table. The city is Bethany and the house is Simon's.

He was known as Simon the leper. But not any longer. Now he is just Simon. We don't know when Jesus healed him. But we do know what he was like before Jesus healed him. Stooped shoulders. Fingerless hand. Scabbed arm and infected back draped in rags. A tattered wrap which hides all of the face except for two screaming white eyes.

But that was before Jesus' touch. Was Simon the one Jesus healed after he delivered the Sermon on the Mount? Was he the one in the ten who returned to say thank-you? Was he one of the four thousand Jesus helped in Bethsaida? Or was he one of the nameless myriads the gospel writers didn't take time to mention?

We don't know. But we know he had Jesus and his disciples over for dinner.

A simple act, but it must have meant a lot to Jesus. After all, the Pharisees are already clearing him a cell on death row. Won't be long until they finger Lazarus as an accomplice. Could be that the whole lot of them will be on wanted posters by the end of the week. It takes nerve to have a wanted man in your home.

But it takes more nerve to put your hand on a leper's sore.

Simon didn't forget what Jesus had done. He couldn't forget. Where there had been a nub, there was now a finger for his daughter to hold. Where there had been ulcerous sores, there was now skin for his wife to stroke. And where there had been lonely hours in quarantine, there were now happy hours such as this—a house full of friends, a table full of food.

No Simon didn't forget. Simon knew what it was like to stare death in the face. He knew what it was like to have no home to call your own and he knew what it was like to be misunderstood. He wanted Jesus to know that if he ever needed a meal and a place to lay his head, there was one house in Bethany to which he could go.

Other homes will not be as gracious as Simon's. Before the week is up, Jesus will spend some time in the High Priest's house, the nicest in Jerusalem. Three barns in the back and a beautiful view of the valley. But Jesus won't see the view, he'll see only the false witnesses, hear the lies, and feel the slaps on his face.

He won't find hospitality in the home of the High Priest.

Before the week is up, Jesus will visit the chambers of Herod. Elegant chambers. Plenty of servants. Perhaps there is fruit and wine on the table. But Herod won't offer any to Jesus. Herod wants a trick. A sideshow. "Show me a miracle, country-boy," he will jab. The guards will snicker.

Before the week is up, Jesus will visit the home of Pilate. Rare opportunity to stand before the couch of the Procurator of all Israel.

Should be an honor. Should be a moment to remember, but it won't be. It's a moment the world would rather forget. Pilate has an opportunity to perform the world's greatest act of mercy—and he doesn't. God is in his house and Pilate doesn't see him.

We can't help but wonder, *What if?* What if Pilate had come to the defense of the innocent? What if Herod had asked Jesus for help and not entertainment? What if the High Priest had been as concerned with truth as he was his position? What if one of them had turned their back on the crowd and their face toward the Christ and made a stand?

But they didn't. The mountain of prestige was too high. The fall would have been too great.

But Simon did. Risky love seizes the moment. Simon took a chance. He gave Jesus a good meal. Not much, but more than most. And when the priests accused and the soldiers slapped, perhaps Jesus remembered what Simon did and was strengthened.

And when he remembered Simon's meal, perhaps he remembered Mary's gesture. Maybe he could even smell the perfume.

Not unlikely that he could. After all it was twelve ounces worth. Imported. Concentrated. Sweet. Strong enough to scent a man's clothes for days.

Between the lashings, I wonder, did he relive the moment? As he hugged the Roman post and braced himself for the next ripping of his back, did he remember the oil which soothed his skin? Could he, in the faces of the women who stared, see the small, soft face of Mary, who cared?

She was the only one who believed him. Whenever he spoke of his death the others shrugged, the others doubted, but Mary believed. Mary believed because he spoke with a firmness she'd heard before.

"Lazarus, come out!" he'd demanded, and her brother came out. After four days in a stone-sealed grave he walked out.

And as Mary kissed the now-warm hands of her just-dead brother, she turned and looked. Jesus was smiling. Tear streaks were dry and the teeth shone from beneath the beard. He was smiling.

And in her heart she knew she would never doubt his words.

So when he spoke of his death, she believed.

And when she saw the three together, she couldn't resist. Simon, the healed leper, head thrown back in laughter. Lazarus, the resurrected corpse, leaning in to see what Jesus has said. And Jesus, the source of life for both, beginning his joke a second time.

"Now is the right time," she told herself.

It wasn't an act of impulse. She'd carried the large vial of perfume from her house to Simon's. It wasn't a spontaneous gesture. But it was an extravagant one. The perfume was worth a year's wages. Maybe the only thing of value she had. It wasn't a logical thing to do, but since when has love been led by logic?

Logic hadn't touched Simon.

Common sense hadn't wept at Lazarus's tomb.

Practicality didn't feed the crowds or love the children. Love did. Extravagant, risky, chance-taking love.

And now someone needs to show the same to the giver of such love.

So Mary did. She stepped up behind him and stood with the jar in her hand. Within a couple of moments every mouth was silent and every eye wide as they watched her nervous fingers remove the ornate cover.

Only Jesus was unaware of her presence. Just as he noticed everyone looking behind him, she began to pour. Over his head. Over his shoulders. Down his back. She would have poured herself out for him if she could.

The fragrance rushed through the room. Smells of cooked lamb and herbs were lost in the aroma of the sweet ointment.

"Wherever you go," the gesture spoke, "breathe the aroma and remember one who cares."

On his skin the fragrance of faith. In his clothing the balm of belief. Even as the soldiers tore his garment in two her gesture brought a bouquet into a cemetery.

The other disciples had mocked her extravagance. They thought it foolish. Ironic. Jesus had saved them from a sinking boat in a stormy sea. He'd enabled them to heal and preach. He'd brought focus into their fuzzy lives. They, the recipients of exorbitant love, chastised her generosity.

"Why waste that perfume? It could have been sold for a great deal of money and given to the poor," they smirk.

Don't miss Jesus' prompt defense of Mary. "Why are you troubling this woman? She has done an excellent thing for me." [1]

Jesus' message is just as powerful today as it was then. Don't miss it: "There is a time for risky love. There is a time for extravagant gestures. There is a time to pour out your affections on one you love. And when the time comes—seize it, don't miss it."

The young husband is packing his wife's belongings. His task solemn. His heart heavy. He never dreamed she would die so young. But the cancer came so sure, so quickly. At the bottom of the drawer he finds a box, a negligee. Unworn. Still wrapped in paper. "She was always waiting for a special occasion," he says to himself, "always waiting. . . ."

As the boy on the bicycle watches the students taunt, he churns inside. That's his little brother they are laughing at. He knows he should step in and stand up for his brother, but . . . those are his friends doing the teasing. What will they think? And because it matters what they think, he turns and pedals away.

As the husband looks in the jewelry case, he rationalizes, "Sure she would want the watch, but it's too expensive. She's a practical woman, she'll understand. I'll just get the bracelet today. I'll buy the watch . . . someday."

Someday. The enemy of risky love is a snake whose tongue has mastered the talk of deception. "Someday," he hisses.

"Someday, I can take her on the cruise."

"Someday, I will have time to call and chat."

"Someday, the children will understand why I was so busy."

But you know the truth, don't you? You know even before I write it. You could say it better than I.

Some days never come.

And the price of practicality is sometimes higher than extravagance.

But the rewards of risky love are always greater than its cost.

Go to the effort. Invest the time. Write the letter. Make the apology. Take the trip. Purchase the gift. Do it. The seized opportunity renders joy. The neglected brings regret.

The reward was great for Simon. He was privileged to give rest to the one who made the earth. Simon's gesture will never be forgotten.

Neither will Mary's. Jesus promised, "Wherever the Good News is preached in all the world, what this woman has done will be told, and people will remember her."[2]

Simon and Mary: Examples of the risky gift given at the right time.

Which brings us back to Artful Eddie, the Chicago mobster who squealed on Al Capone so his son could have a fair chance. Had Eddie lived to see his son Butch grow up, he would have been proud.

He would have been proud of Butch's appointment to Annapolis. He would have been proud of the commissioning as a World War II Navy pilot. He would have been proud as he read of his son downing five bombers in the Pacific night and saving the lives of hundreds of crewmen on the carrier *Lexington*. The name was cleared. The Congressional Medal of Honor which Butch received was proof.

When people say the name O'Hare in Chicago, they don't think gangsters—they think aviation heroism. And now when you say his name, you have something else to think about. Think about the hear it. Think about it the next time you fly into the airport named after the son of a gangster gone good.

The son of Eddie O'Hare.

Chapter 7

The Guy with the Donkey

"If anyone asks you why you are taking the donkeys, say that the Master needs them, and he will send them at once."
Matthew 21:3

When we all get home I know what I want to do. There's someone I want to get to know. You go ahead and swap stories with Mary or talk doctrine with Paul. I'll catch up with you soon. But first, I want to meet the guy with the donkey.

I don't know his name or what he looks like. I only know one thing: what he gave. He gave a donkey to Jesus on the Sunday he entered Jerusalem.

"Go to the town you can see there. When you enter it, you will quickly find a donkey tied there with its colt. Untie them and bring them to me. If anyone asks you why you are taking the donkeys, say that the Master needs them, and he will send them at once."[1]

When we all get to heaven I want to visit this fellow. I have several questions for him.

How did you know? How did you know it was Jesus who needed a donkey? Did you have a vision? Did you get a telegram? Did an angel appear in your bowl of lentil?

Was it hard to give? Was it difficult to give something to Jesus for him to use? I want to ask that question because sometimes it's hard for me. Sometimes I like to keep my animals to myself. Sometimes when God wants something I act like I don't know he needs it.

How did it feel? How did it feel to look out and see Jesus on the back of the donkey that lived in your barn? Were you proud? Were you surprised? Were you annoyed?

Did you know? Did you have any idea that your generosity would be used for such a noble purpose? Did it ever occur to you that God was going to ride your donkey? Were you aware that all four Gospel writers would tell your story? Did it ever cross your mind that a couple of millenniums later, a curious preacher in South Texas would be pondering your plight late at night?

And as I ponder yours, I ponder mine. Sometimes I get the impression that God wants me to give him something and sometimes I don't give it because I don't know for sure, and then I feel bad because I've missed my chance. Other times I know he wants something but I don't give it because I'm too selfish. And other times, too few times, I hear him and I obey him and feel honored that a gift of mine would be used to carry Jesus into another place. And still other times I wonder if my little deeds today will make a difference in the long haul.

Maybe you have those questions, too. All of us have a donkey. You and I each have something in our lives, which, if given back to God, could, like the donkey, move Jesus and his story further down the road. Maybe you can sing or hug or program a computer or speak Swahili or write a check.

Whichever, that's your donkey.

Whichever, your donkey belongs to him.

It really does belong to him. Your gifts are his and the donkey was his. The original wording of the instructions Jesus gave to his disciples is proof: "If anyone asks you why you are taking the donkeys, you are to say, 'Its Lord is in need.' "

The language Jesus used is the language of a royal levy. It was an ancient law which required the citizen to render to the king any item or service he or one of his emissaries might request.[2] In making such a request, Jesus is claiming to be king. He is speaking as one in authority. He is stating that as king he has rights to any possession of his subjects.

It could be that God wants to mount your donkey and enter the walls of another city, another nation, another heart. Do you let him? Do you give it? Or do you hesitate?

That guy who gave Jesus the donkey is just one in a long line of folks who gave little things to a big God. Scripture has quite a gallery of donkey-givers. In fact, heaven may have a shrine to honor God's uncommon use of the common.

It's a place you won't want to miss. Stroll through and see Rahab's rope, Paul's bucket, David's sling, and Samson's jawbone. Wrap your hand around the staff which split the sea and smote the rock. Sniff the ointment which soothed Jesus' skin and lifted his heart. Rest your head on the same cloak which gave comfort to Christ in the boat and run your hand along the smooth wood of the manger, soft as a baby's skin. Or set your shoulder beneath the heavy Roman beam, as coarse as a traitor's kiss.

I don't know if these items will be there. But I am sure of one thing—the people who used them will.

The risk-takers: Rahab who sheltered the spy. The brethren who smuggled Paul.

The conquerors: David, slinging a stone. Samson, swinging a bone. Moses, lifting a rod.

The care-givers: Mary at Jesus' feet. What she gave cost much, but somehow she knew what he would give would cost more.

The anonymous disciple in the boat. He made a bed out of the boat so God could take a nap.

And the curious pilgrim on the side of the Via Dolorosa. For all we know, he knew very little. He just knew Jesus' bloody, beaten back was weary and his own back was strong. So when the soldier pointed, this man came.

Quite a fraternity, is it not? Strong stewards who view what is theirs as his and make it available whenever he might need it. Sharecroppers of the vineyard who haven't forgotten who owns the property. Loyal students who remember who is paying the tuition.

Here's another: A nineteenth-century Sunday school teacher who led a Boston shoe clerk to Christ. The teacher's name you've never heard: Kimball. The name of the shoe clerk he converted you have: Dwight Moody.

Moody became an evangelist and had a major influence on a young preacher named Frederick B. Meyer. Meyer began to preach on college campuses and while doing so, he converted J. Wilbur Chapman. Chapman became involved in the YMCA and arranged for a former baseball player named Billy Sunday to come to Charlotte, North Carolina, for a revival. A group of Charlotte community leaders were so enthusiastic afterward that they planned another campaign and brought Mordecai Hamm to town to preach. In that revival a young man named Billy Graham yielded his life to Christ.

Did the Boston school teacher have any idea what would become of his conversation with the shoe salesman? No, he, like the owner of the donkey, had a chance to help Jesus journey into another heart, so he did.

Some years ago, I was on a campaign in Hawaii. (Hey, somebody has to go to those desolate places!) My job was to go door-to-door and invite people to our nightly meetings. Most of the folks were kind but not too interested. Though no one was rude, no one asked us in either. Then we came upon a lady of grace who is not mentioned in Scripture only because she was born two millenniums too late.

I don't know her name, but I remember her presence—and her presents.

She was a wisp of a lady. Small. Oriental. Shoulders hunched by the years. A woman of modest means, she worked as a maid at one of the many hotels which dot the beach. When she learned we were sharing Christ, she insisted we come into her house and see how she was trying to influence her co-workers. Into a back room we went. In it was a large table covered with decoupage material. Glue. Paint. Wooden frames.

But most of the space was taken up by pieces of wood which were carved to look like an open wooden book.

She explained that she couldn't read, so it would be difficult for her to teach. She explained that she had little income, so it would be impossible to give money. But somewhere she had learned this craft and was now using it to introduce her faith to her friends. Her plan was simple. She took the wooden book and on one side of it pasted a Polaroid picture of her friend. On the other she put a Bible verse.

Her rationale? People love to see a picture of themselves. Most of her friends were simple folks with few wall decorations. Here was a way to hang a Bible verse on their wall where they would see it every day. Would something come of it? You never know.

But God does. God uses tiny seeds to reap great harvests. It is on the back of donkeys he rides—not steeds or chariots—just simple donkeys.

If I had asked my questions to the Hawaiian lady she would have answered, "He always needs us. We are his mouth. We are his hands." I can see her blush, honored that her gifts would be chosen by a king.

I wouldn't have had to ask, "Is it hard? Is it hard to give?" The answer was in her smile.

And that last question. No, I wouldn't have to ask it either. "Do you think that two thousand years from now . . ." She has no way of knowing. The guy with the donkey didn't. Samson didn't. Moses and Rahab didn't. The shoe salesman didn't, and we don't either. No sower of small seeds can know the extent of his harvest.

But don't be surprised if in heaven, next to David's sling and Moses' rod and the donkey's rope you discover a decoupaged book with a picture and a verse.

Chapter 8

Hucksters
and
Hypocrites

*"My Temple will be called a house for prayer.
But you are changing it into a 'hideout for robbers.'"*
Matthew 21:13

*S*peedy Morris is the basketball coach for LaSalle University.
He was shaving when his wife told him he was wanted on the
phone by *Sports Illustrated*. He got so excited over the prospect of
national recognition that he hurried his shave and nicked himself.
Not wanting to delay the caller, he ran out of the bathroom, lost his
balance, and tumbled down the stairs. Limping, with blood and
lather on his face, he finally got to the phone.

"Sports Illustrated?" he panted.

Imagine Morris's disappointment when the voice on the other
end droned, "Yes it is, and for seventy-five cents an issue you can
get a year's subscription. . . ." [1]

It's tough to be let down. It's disappointing when you think
someone is interested in you, only to find they are interested in your
money. When salespeople do it, it's irritating—but when people of
faith do it, it can be devastating.

It's a sad but true fact of the faith: religion is used for profit and prestige. When it is there are two results: people are exploited and God is infuriated.

There's no better example of this than what happened at the temple. After he had entered the city on the back of a donkey, Jesus "went into the Temple. After he had looked at everything, since it was already late, he went out to Bethany with the twelve apostles."[2]

Did you catch that? The first place Jesus went when he arrived in Jerusalem was the temple. He'd just been paraded through the streets and treated like a king. It was Sunday, the first day of the Passover week. Hundreds of thousands of people packed the narrow stone streets. Rivers of pilgrims flooded the marketplace. Jesus elbowed his way through the sea of people as evening was about to fall. He walked into the temple area, looked around, and walked out.

Want to know what he saw? Then read what he did on Monday, the next morning when he returned. "Jesus went into the Temple and threw out all the people who were buying and selling there. He turned over the tables of those who were exchanging different kinds of money, and he upset the benches of those who were selling doves. Jesus said to all the people there, 'It is written in the Scriptures, "My temple will be called a house for prayer." But you are changing it into a "hideout for robbers." ' "[3]

What did he see? Hucksters. Faith peddlers. What lit the fire under Jesus' broiler? What was his first thought on Monday? People in the temple making a franchise out of the faith.

It was Passover week. The Passover was the highlight of the Jewish calendar. People came from all regions and many countries to be present for the celebration. Upon arriving they were obligated to meet two requirements.

First, an animal sacrifice, usually a dove. The dove had to be perfect, without blemish. The animal could be brought in from anywhere, but odds were that if you brought a sacrifice from another place, yours would be considered insufficient by the authorities in the temple. So, under the guise of keeping the sacrifice pure, the dove sellers sold doves—at their price.

Second, the people had to pay a tax, a temple tax. It was due every year. During Passover the tax had to be rendered in local currency. Knowing many foreigners would be in Jerusalem to pay the tax, money changers conveniently set up tables and offered to exchange the foreign money for local—for a modest fee, of course.

It's not difficult to see what angered Jesus. Pilgrims journeyed days to see God, to witness the holy, to worship His Majesty. But before they were taken into the presence of God, they were taken to the cleaners. What was promised and what was delivered were two different things.

Want to anger God? Get in the way of people who want to see him. Want to feel his fury? Exploit people in the name of God.

Mark it down. Religious hucksters poke the fire of divine wrath.

"I've had enough," was written all over the Messiah's face. In he stormed. Doves flapped and tables flew. People scampered and traders scattered.

This was not an impulsive show. This was not a temper tantrum. It was a deliberate act with an intentional message. Jesus had seen the money-changers the day before. He went to sleep with pictures of this midway and its barkers in his memory. And when he woke up the next morning, knowing his days were drawing to a close, he chose to make a point: "You cash in on my people and you've got me to answer to." God will never hold guiltless those who exploit the privilege of worship.

Some years ago I was in the Miami airport to pick up a friend. As I walked through the terminal, a convert of an Eastern cult got my attention.

You know the kind I'm talking about: beads, sandals, frozen smile, backpack of books.

"Sir," she said. (I should have kept walking.)

"Sir, just a moment, please." Well, I had a moment. I was early and the plane was late, so what harm? (I should have kept walking.)

I stopped and she began her spiel. She said she was a teacher and her school was celebrating an anniversary. In honor of the event, they were giving away a book which explained their philosophy. She placed a copy in my hand. It was a thick hardback with a mystic cover. A guru-looking guy was sitting cross-legged with his hands folded.

I thanked her for the book and began to walk away.

"Sir?" I stopped. I knew what was coming.

"Would you like to make a donation to our school?"

"No," I responded, "but thanks for the book."

I began to walk away. She followed me and tapped me on the shoulder.

"Sir, everyone so far has given a donation in appreciation for the gift."

"That's good," I replied, "but I don't think I will. But I appreciate the book." I turned and began to walk away. I hadn't even taken a step, however, when she spoke again. This time she was agitated.

"Sir," and she opened her purse so I could see her collection of dollars and coins. "If you were sincere in your gratitude you would give a donation in appreciation."

That was low. That was sneaky. Insulting. I'm not usually terse, but I couldn't resist. "That may be true," I responded, "but if you were sincere, you wouldn't give me a gift and then ask me to pay for it."

She reached for the book, but I tucked it under my arm and walked away.

A small victory against the mammoth of hucksterism.

Sadly, the hucksters win more than they lose. And, even more sadly, hucksters garb themselves in Christian costumes as much as those of Eastern cults.

You've seen them. The talk is smooth. The vocabulary eloquent. The appearance genuine. They are on your television. They are on your radio. They may even be in your pulpit.

May I speak candidly?

The time has come to tolerate religious hucksters no longer. These seekers of "sanctimoney" have stained the reputation of Christianity. They have muddied the altars and shattered the stained glass. They manipulate the easily deceived. They are not governed by God; they are governed by greed. They are not led by the Spirit; they are propelled by pride. They are marshmallow phonies who excel in emotion and fail in doctrine. They strip-mine faith to get a dollar and rape the pew to get a payment. Our master unveiled their scams and so must we.

How? By recognizing them. Two trademarks give them away. One, they emphasize their profit more than the Prophet.

In the church in Crete some people made a living off the gullible souls in the church. Paul had strong words about them. "These people must be stopped, because they are upsetting whole families by teaching things they should not teach, which they do to get rich by cheating people."[4]

Listen carefully to the television evangelist. Analyze the words of the radio preacher. Note the emphasis of the message. What is the burden? Your salvation or your donation? Monitor what is said. Is money always needed yesterday? Are you promised health if you give and hell if you don't? If so, ignore him.

A second characteristic of ecclesiastical con men: they build more fences than they build faith.

Medicine men tell you to stay out of the pharmacy. They don't want you trying other treatments. Neither do hucksters. They present themselves as pioneers that the mainline church couldn't stomach, but, in reality, they are lone wolves on the prowl.

They have franchised an approach and want to protect it. Their bread and butter is the uniqueness of their faith. Only they can give you what you need. Their cure-all kit is the solution to your aches. Just as the dove-sellers were intolerant of imported birds, the hucksters are wary of imported faith.

Their aim is to cultivate a clientele of loyal checkbooks.

"Look out for those who cause people to be against each other and who upset other people's faith. They are against the true teaching you learned, so stay away from them. Such people are not serving our Lord Christ but are only doing what pleases themselves. They use fancy talk and fine words to fool the minds of those who do not know about evil."[5]

Christ's passion on Monday is indignance. For that reason I make no apology about challenging you to call the cards on these guys. God has been calling a halt to babblers building towers for centuries. So should we.

If not, it could happen again.

No one ever expected it would happen the first time. Especially with this church. It was the model congregation. A heated swimming pool was made available for underprivileged kids. Horses were provided for inner city children to ride. The church gave scholarships and provided housing for senior citizens. It even had an animal shelter and medical facility, an out-patient care facility, and a drug rehabilitation program.

Walter Mondale wrote that the pastor was an "inspiration to us all." The Secretary of Health, Education, and Welfare cited the pastor's outstanding contribution. We are told "he knew how to inspire hope. He was committed to people in need, he counseled prisoners and juvenile delinquents. He started a job placement center; he opened rest homes and homes for the retarded; he had a health clinic; he organized a vocational training center; he provided free legal aid; he founded a community center; he preached about God. He even claimed to cast out demons, do miracles, and heal."[6]

Lofty words. A lengthy resume for what appeared to be a

mighty spiritual leader and his church. Where is that congregation today? What is she doing now?

The church is dead . . . literally.

Death occurred the day the pastor called the members to the pavilion. They heard his hypnotic voice over the speaker system and from all corners of the farm they came. He sat in his large chair and spoke into a hand-held microphone about the beauty of death and the certainty that they would meet again.

The people were surrounded by armed guards. A vat of cyanide-laced Kool-Aid was brought out. Most of the cult members drank the poison with no resistance. Those who did resist were forced to drink.

First, the babies and children—about eighty—were given the fatal drink. Then the adults—women and men, leaders and followers, and finally the pastor.

Everything was calm for a few minutes, then the convulsions began, screams filled the Guyana sky, mass confusion broke out. In a few minutes, it was over. The members of the Peoples Temple Christian Church were all dead. All 780 of them.

And so was their leader, Jim Jones.

Mark it down and beware: there are hucksters in God's house. Don't be fooled by their looks. Don't be dazzled by their words. Be careful. Remember why Jesus purged the temple. Those closest to it may be the farthest from it.

Chapter 9

Courage to Dream Again

"If you have faith, it will happen."
Matthew 21:21

Hans Babblinger of Ulm, Germany, wanted to fly. He wanted to break the bond of gravity. He wanted to soar like a bird.

Problem: He lived in the sixteenth century. There were no planes, no helicopters, no flying machines. He was a dreamer born too soon. What he wanted was impossible.

Hans Babblinger, however, made a career out of helping people overcome the impossible. He made artificial limbs. In his day amputation was a common cure for disease and injury, so he kept busy. His task was to help the handicapped overcome circumstance.

Babblinger longed to do the same for himself.

With time, he used his skills to construct a set of wings. The day soon came to try them out and he tested his wings in the foothills of the Bavarian Alps. Good choice. Lucky choice. Up currents are common in the region. On a memorable day with friends watching and sun shining, he jumped off an embankment and soared safely down.

His heart raced. His friends applauded. And God rejoiced.

How do I know God rejoiced? Because God always rejoices when we dare to dream. In fact, we are much like God when we dream. The Master exults in newness. He delights in stretching the old. He wrote the book on making the impossible possible.

Examples? Check the Book.

Eighty-year-old shepherds don't usually play chicken with Pharaohs . . . but don't tell that to Moses.

Teenage shepherds don't normally have showdowns with giants . . . but don't tell that to David.

Night-shift shepherds don't usually get to hear angels sing and see God in a stable . . . but don't tell that to the Bethlehem bunch.

And for sure don't tell that to God. He's made an eternity out of making the earthbound airborne. And he gets angry when people's wings are clipped. Such is the message of the fig tree drama, a peculiar scene involving a fruitless fig tree and a mountain in the ocean.

Jesus and his disciples walked to Jerusalem on Monday morning after spending the night in Bethany. He was hungry and saw a fig tree on the side of the road. As he approached the tree, he noticed that though it had leaves, it had no fruit. Something about a tree with no fruit reminded him of what he saw in the temple on Sunday and what he is going to do in the temple later that day.[1]

So he denounced the tree. "You will never again have fruit." The tree immediately dried up.

The next day, Tuesday, the disciples see what has happened to the tree. They are amazed. Just twenty-four hours before, the tree had been green and healthy; now it is barren and dry.

"How did the fig tree dry up so quickly?" they ask.

Jesus gives them this answer, "I tell you the truth, if you have faith and do not doubt, you will be able to do what I did to this tree and even more. You will be able to say to this mountain, 'Go, fall into the sea.' And if you have faith, it will happen. If you believe, you will get anything you ask for in prayer."[2]

You won't find the words *dream* or *fly* or *wing* in the story. But look closely and you'll see a story of a God who issues a call for the Babblingers of the world to mount the cliff and test their wings. You'll also see a God who scorns those who put dreamers in a cage and pocket the key.

Jesus, hungry and on his way to Jerusalem, stops to see if a fig tree has figs. It doesn't. It has the appearance of nutrition but offers nothing. It's all promise and no performance. The symbolism is too precise for Jesus to ignore.

He does to the tree on Monday morning what he will do to the temple on Monday afternoon: He curses it. Note, he's not angry at the tree. He's angry at what the tree represents. Jesus is disgusted by lukewarm, placid, vain believers who have pomp but no purpose. They have no fruit. This simple act slams the guillotine on the neck of empty religion.

Want a graphic example of this? Consider the Laodicean church. This church was wealthy and self-sufficient. But the church had a problem—hollow, fruitless faith. "I know what you do," God spoke to this group, "that you are not hot nor cold. I wish that you were hot or cold! But because you are lukewarm—neither hot, nor cold—I am ready to spit you out of my mouth."[3]

The literal translation is "to vomit." Why does the body vomit something? Why does it recoil violently at the presence of certain substances? Because they are incompatible with the body. Vomiting is the body's way of rejecting anything it cannot handle.

What's the point? God can't stomach lukewarm faith. He is angered by a religion that puts on a show but ignores the service— and that is precisely the religion he was facing during his last week. And the religion he had faced his entire ministry.

When he served they complained.

They complained that his disciples ate on the wrong day. They complained that he healed on the wrong day. They complained that he forgave the wrong people. They complained that he hung out with the wrong crowd and had the wrong influence on the children. But, still worse, every time he tried to set people free, the religious leaders attempted to tie them down. Those closest to the temple were quickest with the shackles. When a courageous soul tried to fly they were there to say it couldn't be done.

By the way, they told Hans Babblinger the same thing. Seems the king was coming to Ulm and the Bishop and the citizens wanted to impress him. Word had gotten out about Hans's flying feat so they asked him to do a loop for the king. Hans consented.

They wanted one change, however. Since the crowd would be large and the hills were difficult to climb, could Hans choose a place in the lowlands in which he could fly?

Hans chose the bluffs near the Danube. They were broad and flat and the river was a good distance below. He would jump off the edge and float down to the water.

Poor choice. The updraft in the hills was nonexistent near the river. So in front of the king, his court, and half the village, Hans jumped and fell like a rock straight into the river. The king was disappointed and the Bishop mortified.

Guess what the Bishop preached the next Sunday—"Man was not meant to fly." Hans believed him. Imprisoned by a pulpit he put his wings away and never again tried to fly. He died soon after, gripped by gravity, buried with his dreams.

The cathedral of Ulm isn't the first church to cage a flyer. Through the years pulpits have grown proficient in telling people what they can't do. They did in the day of Christ, they did in the day of Hans Babblinger, and they do today—and you can be sure it is just as nauseating to God today as it was then.

But as we are looking at religion, we would do well to look in the mirror. You see, it is convenient to point fingers at organized religion and say, "Amen. Tell 'em like it is!" It's comfortable to do that, but inadequate. While we are talking about setting people free to fly, think about yourself. How are you at giving wings? How have you been at setting people free?

That friend who offended you and needs your forgiveness?
The co-worker burdened with fear of the grave?
The relative who carries the sack of yesterday's failures?
Your friend weighed down by anxiety?
Tell them about the empty tomb . . . and watch them fly.

A Hispanic member of our church married recently. She is a precious sister with a robust faith. When the time came, the minister asked, "Can you repeat the vows?" To which she answered with all sincerity, "Yes, I can, but it will be with an accent."

That is the way God intended it. He intends for each of us to live out his vows but with our own particular accent. For some, it is with an accent on the sick. For others, it is a concern for the imprisoned. Still others have a burden for scholarly research or giving. But whatever our accent the message is still the same.

The message of the fig tree is not for all of us to have the same fruit. The message is for us to have some fruit. Not easy. Jesus knows that. "If you have faith and do not doubt, you will be able to do what I did to this tree and even more."

Faith in whom? Religion? Hardly. Religion is the hoax Jesus is out to disclose. In fact, when Jesus said, "You will be able to say to this mountain, 'Go, fall into the sea,' " he was probably looking up from the Kidron Valley to the Temple Mount—the temple known to many as Mount Zion. If that is the case, you have reason to smile as Jesus tells you what to do with the church that tries to cage your flight, "Tell it to jump into the lake."

No, the faith is not in religion, the faith is in God. A hardy, daring faith which believes God will do what is right, every time. And that God will do what it takes—whatever it takes—to bring his children home.

He is the shepherd in search of his lamb. His legs are scratched, his feet are sore and his eyes are burning. He scales the cliffs and traverses the fields. He explores the caves. He cups his hands to his mouth and calls into the canyon.

And the name he calls is yours.

He is the housewife in search of the lost coin. No matter that he has nine others, he won't rest until he has found the tenth. He searches the house. He moves furniture. He pulls up rugs. He cleans out the shelves. He stays up late. He gets up early. All other tasks can wait. Only one matters. The coin is of great value to him. He owns it. He will not stop until he finds it.

The coin he seeks is you.

God is the father pacing the porch. His eyes are wide with his quest. His heart is heavy. He seeks his prodigal. He searches the horizon. He examines the skyline; yearning for the familiar figure, the recognizable gait. His concern is not his business, his investments, his ownings. His concern is the son who wears his name, the child who bears his image. You.

He wants you home.

It is only in light of such passion that we can understand this incredible promise: "If you believe, you will get anything you ask for in prayer."[4]

Don't reduce this grand statement to the category of new cars and paychecks. Don't limit the promise of this passage to the selfish pool of perks and favors. The fruit God assures is far greater than earthly wealth. His dreams are much greater than promotions and proposals.

God wants you to fly. He wants you to fly free of yesterday's guilt. He wants you to fly free of today's fears. He wants you to fly free of tomorrow's grave. Sin, fear, and death. These are the mountains he has moved. These are the prayers he will answer. That is the fruit he will grant. This is what he longs to do: he longs to set you free so you can fly . . . fly home.

One final word about the church of Ulm. It's empty. Now most of its visitors are tourists. And how do most of the tourists travel to Ulm?

They fly.

Chapter 10

Of Calluses and Compassion

"The kingdom of God will be taken away from you and given to people who do the things God wants in his kingdom."
Matthew 21:43

*P*eculiar, this childhood church memory of mine.

For many, early church recollections are made of zippered Bibles, patent leather Easter shoes, Christmas pageants, or Sunday schools. Mine is not so religious. Mine is comprised of calluses, straight pins, and dull sermons.

There I sit, all six years of me, flat-topped and freckled. My father's hand in my lap. It is there to keep me from squirming. A robust preacher is behind the pulpit, one of God's kindest but most monotonous servants. Bored, I turn my attention to my father's hand.

If you didn't know he was a mechanic, one look at his hands would tell you as much. Thick, strong, scrubbed clean but still bearing traces of last week's grease.

I'm intrigued as I run my fingers over the calluses. They rise on the palm like a ridge of hills. Calluses. Layer upon layer of nerveless skin. The hand's defense against hours of squeezing wrenches and twisting screwdrivers.

On the back of the pew in front of me is a collection of

attendance cards. At the top of each card is a red ribbon for the visitors to wear. The ribbon is attached to the card by a straight pin.

I have an idea. *I wonder how thick those calluses are?* . . .

I take the pin, and with the skill of a surgeon I begin the insertion. (I told you it was peculiar.) I look up at Dad. He doesn't move. I go deeper. No response. Another eighth of an inch. No flinch. While the rest of the church is intent on the words of a preacher, I'm fascinated by the depth of a callus. I decide to give it a final shove.

"Umph," he grunts, yanking his hand away, closing his fist which only pushes the pin further. His glares at me, my mother turns, and my brother giggles. Something tells me that the same hand will be used later that Sunday to make another point.

Peculiar, this childhood memory. But, even more peculiar is that three decades later, I find myself doing the same thing I did at age six: in church, trying to penetrate calluses with a point. Only now I'm in the pulpit, not the pew. And my tool is truth, not a pin. And the calluses are not on the hand, but on the heart.

Thick, dead skin wrapped around the nerves of the soul. The result of hours of rubbing against the truth without receiving it. Toughened, crusty, lifeless tissue which defies feeling and ignores touch.

The calloused heart.

To such hearts Jesus spoke on his last Tuesday. With the persistence of a man with one final message, his point was intended to prick the soul.

He told two stories which contain a common thread, crimson with guilt: the proclivity of people to reject God's invitation not once or twice, but time and time again.

The first story was that of the landowner.[1] He leased a vineyard to some sharecroppers and, at harvest, sent his servants to collect his share of the grapes. "But the farmers grabbed the servants, beat one, killed another, and then killed a third servant with stones."

The second is the story of the king who prepared a wedding feast for his son.[2] "When the feast was ready, the king sent his servants to tell the people, but they refused to come."

A landowner whose servants are beaten and killed? A king whose messengers are ignored? Surely the landowner and the king will wash their hands of these people. No doubt they will send the police and the military next.

Wrong.

In both cases they send more emissaries. "So the [landowner] sent some other servants to the farmers, even more than he sent the first time. But the farmers did the same thing to the servants that they had done before."

"Then the king sent other servants, saying, 'Tell those who have been invited that my feast is ready.' "

What surprising tolerance! What unexpected patience! Servant after servant. Messenger after messenger. Jesus verbally painting the picture of a determined God.

When our oldest daughter, Jenna, was two, I lost her in a department store. One minute she was at my side and the next she was gone. I panicked. All of a sudden only one thing mattered—I had to find my daughter. Shopping was forgotten. The list of things I came to get was unimportant. I yelled her name. What people thought didn't matter. For a few minutes, every ounce of energy had one goal—to find my lost child. (I did, by the way. She was hiding behind some jackets!)

No price is too high for a parent to pay to redeem his child. No energy is too great. No effort too demanding. A parent will go to any length to find his or her own.

So will God.

Mark it down. God's greatest creation is not the flung stars or the gorged canyons, it's his eternal plan to reach his children. Behind his pursuit of us is the same brilliance behind the rotating seasons and the orbiting planets. Heaven and earth know no greater passion than God's personal passion for you and your return. Through holy surprises he has made his faithfulness clear.

Noah saw it as the clouds opened and the rainbow appeared. Abram felt it as he placed his hand on aging Sarai's belly. Jacob found it through failure. Joseph experienced it in prison. Pharaoh heard it through Moses.

"Let my people go."

But Pharaoh refused. As a result, he was given a front-row seat in the arena of divine devotion. Water became blood. The day became night. Locusts came. Children died. The Red Sea opened. The Egyptian army drowned.

Listen to these seldom read but impassioned words of Moses as he speaks to the Israelites. "Nothing like this has ever happened before! Look at the past, long before you were even born. Go all the way back to when God made humans on the earth, and look from one end of heaven to the other. Nothing like this has ever been heard of! No other people have ever heard God speak from a fire and have still lived. But you have. No other god has ever taken for himself one nation out of another. But the LORD your God did this for you in Egypt, right before your own eyes. He did it with tests, signs, miracles, war, and great sights, by his great power and strength."[3]

Moses' message? God will change the world to reach the world. God is tireless, relentless. He refuses to quit.

Listen as God articulates his passion: "My heart beats for you, and my love for you stirs up my pity. I won't punish you in my anger, and I won't destroy Israel again. I am God and not a human; I am the Holy One, and I am among you."[4]

Before you read any further, reflect on those last four words, "I am among you." Do you believe that? Do you believe God is near? He wants you to. He wants you to know he is in the midst of your world. Wherever you are as you read these words, he is present. In your car. On the plane. In your office, your bedroom, your den. He's near.

And he is more than near. He is active. Noah's God is your God. The promise given to Abram is given to you. The finger witnessed in Pharaoh's world is moving in yours.

God is in the thick of things in your world. He has not taken up residence in a distant galaxy. He has not removed himself from history. He has not chosen to seclude himself on a throne in an incandescent castle.

He has drawn near. He has involved himself in the car pools, heartbreaks, and funeral homes of our day. He is as near to us on Monday as on Sunday. In the school room as in the sanctuary. At the coffee break as much as the communion table.

Why? Why did God do it? What was his reason?

Some time ago Denalyn was gone for a couple of days and left me alone with the girls. Though the time was not without the typical children's quarrels and occasional misbehavior, it went fine.

"How were the girls?" Denalyn asked when she got home.

"Good. No problem at all."

Jenna overheard my response. "We weren't good, Daddy," she objected. "We fought once, we didn't do what you said once. We weren't good. How can you say we were good?"

Jenna and I had different perceptions of what pleases a father. She thought it depended upon what she did. It didn't. We think the same about God. We think his love rises and falls with our performance. It doesn't. I don't love Jenna for what she does. I love her for whose she is. She is mine.

God loves you for the same reason. He loves you for whose you are, you are his child.[5] It was this love that pursued the Israelites. It was this love that sent the prophets. It was this love which wrapped itself in human flesh and descended the birth canal of Mary. It was this love which walked the hard trails of Galilee and spoke to the hard hearts of the religious.

"This is not normal, Lord GOD," David exclaimed as he considered God's love.[6] You are right, David. God's love is not normal love. It's not normal to love a murderer and adulterer, but God did when he loved David. It isn't normal to love a man who takes his eyes off you, but such was God's love for Solomon.[7] It isn't normal to love people who love stone idols more than they love you, but God did when he refused to give up on Israel.

And it was this love that Jesus was describing on his last Tuesday. The same love which, on Friday, would take him to the cross.

The cross, the zenith of history. All of the past pointed to it and all of the future would depend upon it. It's the great triumph of heaven: God is on the earth. And it is the great tragedy of earth: man has rejected God.

The religious leaders knew Jesus was speaking about them. Just as their fathers had rejected the prophets, now they were rejecting the Prophet—God himself.

Jesus spoke to those who had turned their backs on history. He spoke to those who had blatantly ignored sign after sign, servant after servant. It wasn't as if they had just skipped a paragraph or missed a punchline. It wasn't as if they had misunderstood a chapter. They had missed the whole book. God had come into their city, walked down their street, knocked on their door, and they refused to let him in.

For that reason—because they had refused to believe—Jesus speaks the most sobering words in the Gospel of Matthew: "The kingdom of God will be taken away from you and given to people who do the things God wants in his kingdom."[8]

God is intolerant of the calloused heart.

He is patient with our mistakes. He is longsuffering with our stumbles. He doesn't get angry at our questions. He doesn't turn away when we struggle. But when we repeatedly reject his message, when we are insensitive to his pleadings, when he changes history itself to get our attention and we still don't listen, he honors our request.

"You refuse to listen," Paul said to the Jews. "You are judging yourselves not worthy of having eternal life! So we will now go to the people of other nations."[9]

Note it was not God who made the people unworthy. It was their refusal to listen that excluded them from grace. Jesus condemns the cold heart, the soul so overgrown with self and selfishness that it would blaspheme the source of hope, the heart so evil that it would see the Prince of Peace and call him the Lord of the Flies.[10]

Such blasphemy is unforgivable, not because of God's unwillingness to forgive, but man's unwillingness to seek forgiveness. The calloused heart is the cursed heart. The calloused heart represents the eyes who won't see the obvious and the ears who won't hear the plain. As a result, they do not seek God and pardon will not be given because pardon will not be sought.

Perhaps my childhood memory is not so peculiar after all. In a way it is the story of the gospel: Jesus piercing his hands in order to prick our hearts. Why did God pierce his hands? Why has he been so devoted? Why has he delivered his children and rescued his people?

Let two men who wrote at two ends of your Bible answer that question. First, Moses. You've already read his answer, "So you would know that the LORD is God."[11] Thousands of years, hundreds of messengers, countless miracles, and one bloody cross later, the apostle Paul says the same thing: "God is kind to you so you will change your hearts and lives."[12]

The purpose of his patience? Our repentance.

We began this chapter with one childhood church memory; we'll conclude with another. It is the memory I have of Holman Hunt's painting of Jesus. Perhaps you've seen it. Stone archway . . . ivy-covered bricks . . . Jesus standing before a heavy wooden door.

It was in a Bible I often held as a young boy. Beneath the painting were the words, "Behold, I stand at the door, and knock: if any man hear my voice, and open the door, I will come in to him."[13]

Years later I read about a surprise in the painting. Holman Hunt had intentionally left out something which only the most careful eye would note as missing. I had not noticed it. When I was told about it I went back and looked. Sure enough, it wasn't there. There was no doorknob on the door. It could only be opened from the inside. Hunt's message was the same as this chapter's. The same as God's. The same as all of history.

God comes to your house, steps up to the door, and knocks. But it's up to you to let him in.

Chapter 11

You're Invited

I am writing this as I sit in a large room in the county courthouse of San Antonio, Texas. I am here by invitation. A summons to jury duty. It wasn't too personal. It wasn't very fancy. Just a simple card with my name and directions to the courthouse. But it was an invitation for me and about a hundred other folks to visit the judge.

This certainly isn't the most meaningful invitation in my life, but still it's an invitation. It makes me think of some others in which I've played a part.

Some years back I offered a person a very special invitation. I asked Denalyn to marry me. Being that marriage proposals are not something you give every day, I tried to make the event memorable.

I began by ordering Chinese food from our favorite Chinese restaurant. I ordered our favorite meal—sweet and sour pork. I put in a special request for extra fortune cookies. While the food was being delivered to my apartment, I took a small strip of paper and printed my proposal. When the food arrived I put the paper in the cookie, set the table, put on my best clothes, and waited for Denalyn.

The night was wrapped in romance. Soft music. Candlelight. When she saw the cloth napkins she knew I had something special in mind, but she wasn't sure what. I ate little. The butterflies in my stomach left little room for food. I couldn't wait to get to the dessert, for in the dessert awaited the invitation.

When the moment came for the cookies, she said she wasn't hungry. I had to beg her to take a cookie. I told her if she didn't eat it, at least read her fortune. She did. She opened the cookie and read the words I'd written on the piece of paper.

She began to cry.

I was devastated: I thought I had offended her. I thought I had insulted her. I don't know how I expected her to react, but I never expected her to cry. (That shows how little I knew about women. I now understand that crying is the utility infielder of the emotion—it covers all bases: sorrow, happiness, excitement.)

Happily, hers were tears of excitement. And she said yes. (She has since, however, been reluctant to open any more fortune cookies.)

Invitations are special. Some are casual such as asking for a date. Some are significant such as offering someone a job. Others are permanent, such as proposing marriage. But all are special.

Invitations. Words embossed on a letter: "You are invited to a gala celebrating the grand opening of . . ." Requests received in the mail: "Mr. and Mrs. John Smith request your presence at the wedding of their daughter . . ." Surprises over the phone: "Hey, Joe. I've got an extra ticket to the game. Interested?"

To receive an invitation is to be honored—to be held in high esteem. For that reason all invitations deserve a kind and thoughtful response.

But the most incredible invitations are not found in envelopes or fortune cookies, they are found in the Bible. You can't read about

God without finding him issuing invitations. He invited Eve to marry Adam, the animals to enter the ark, David to be king, Israel to leave bondage, Nehemiah to rebuild Jerusalem. God is an inviting God. He invited Mary to birth his son, the disciples to fish for men, the adulteress woman to start over, and Thomas to touch his wounds. God is the King who prepares the palace, sets the table, and invites his subjects to come in.

In fact, it seems his favorite word is *come.*

"*Come,* let us talk about these things. Though your sins are like scarlet, they can be as white as snow."[1]

"All you who are thirsty, *come* and drink."[2]

"*Come* to me all, all of you who are tired and have heavy loads, and I will give you rest."[3]

"*Come* to the wedding feast."[4]

"*Come* follow me, and I will make you fish for people."[5]

"Let anyone who is thirsty *come* to me and drink."[6]

God is a God who invites. God is a God who calls. God is a God who opens the door and waves his hand pointing pilgrims to a full table.

His invitation is not just for a meal, however, it is for life. An invitation to come into his kingdom and take up residence in a tearless, graveless, painless world. Who can come? Whoever wishes. The invitation is at once universal and personal.

In the last week of his life, Jesus offered two stories about urgent invitations.

The first is about two sons whose father invited them to work in the vineyard.[7] Their invitations are identical; their responses opposite. One says no, then changes his mind and goes. The other says yes, then changes his mind and stays.

The second story is about a king who prepared a wedding feast for his son.[8] He invited the people to come, but they didn't. Some ignored the invitation, some gave excuses about being too busy, others actually killed the servants bearing the invitation.

Have you ever wondered how Jesus felt as he told these stories? If you've ever had a personal invitation ignored, you know how he felt. Most people don't reject Jesus . . . they just don't give his invitation serious thought.

Imagine my feelings had Denalyn responded to me the way many respond to God. What if she had been vague and noncommittal? Imagine me on the edge of my seat watching her read the proposal in the amber of the candlelight. What if, instead of tears, she had given me idle talk.

"Oh, marriage has been in our family for years."

"What?"

"Marriage has been in our family for years. My uncle got married. My aunt got married. My mom and dad. I even have a sister . . ."

"Wait, wait, wait. What does this have to do with us? I'm talking about you and me."

"Well, Max, like I say, I'm all in favor of marriage. I think it's a wonderful idea, a terrific institution."

"But I'm not asking for your opinion on an institution, I'm asking for your hand in marriage."

It must sadden the Father when we give him vague responses to his specific invitation to come to him. "How kind of you to invite me, Jesus. You know my family has always been religious. In fact we trace our roots back to the Huguenot revolution. You probably remember my great-great-uncle Horace? He was a priest and real popular with the Indians."

"What?"

"Like I say, our family has been pro-religion for years. My Aunt Macy sang in the choir at First Baptist and my cousin Arnold is a deacon at . . ."

It was to such ramblings that God spoke these words in Jeremiah 7:13, "I spoke to you again and again, but you did not listen to me. I called you, but you did not answer."

What if Denalyn had said, "Max, you are very kind to think of me, but could we talk about this tomorrow? There is a movie coming on TV in a few minutes which I really want to see."

Or, even worse.

"Marriage? Well, you know Max, we ought to discuss that someday. Let me see, I've got an opening next . . . no that's not a good day . . . how about two weeks from Tuesday? You give me a call and we'll set up a time."

Oh, that would hurt. You see, it's one thing to be rejected. It's another not to be taken seriously. Nothing stabs deeper than to give a once-in-a-million, for-your-eyes-only invitation and have it relegated to a list of decisions to be made next week.

Jesus gives the invitation. "Here I am! I stand at the door and knock."[9] To know God is to receive his invitation. Not just to hear it, not just to study it, not just to acknowledge it, but to receive it. It is possible to learn much about God's invitation and never respond to it personally.

Yet his invitation is clear and non-negotiable. He gives all and we give him all. Simple and absolute. He is clear in what he asks and clear in what he offers. The choice is up to us.

Isn't it incredible that God leaves the choice to us? Think about it. There are many things in life we can't choose. We can't, for example, choose the weather. We can't control the economy.

We can't choose whether or not we are born with a big nose or blue eyes or a lot of hair. We can't even choose how people respond to us.

But we can choose where we spend eternity. The big choice, God leaves to us. The critical decision is ours.

What are you doing with God's invitation?

What are you doing with his personal request that you live with him forever?

That is the only decision which really matters. Whether or not you take the job transfer is not critical. Whether or not you buy a new car is not crucial. What college you choose or what profession you select is important, but not compared to where you spend eternity. That is the decision you will remember.

What are you doing with his invitation?

As I said earlier, I write as I wait in a large room of our county courthouse. I am here by invitation. As I look around me, I see a hundred or so strangers who also received the same jury summons. They read magazines. They flip through newspapers. They stand and stretch. They do office work. And I ponder the irony of finishing a chapter on God's invitation in a room where I wait for the judge to call my name.

Every few minutes the muffled conversations are silenced by an official-looking gentleman who will enter the room and call names: Yvonne Campbell, Johnny Solis, Thomas Adams. Those he calls will be given instructions and the rest of us return to our activities.

I'm apprehensive about the interview: I don't know what the judge will do. I don't know what the judge will ask. I don't know what the judge will require. I don't know what the outcome will be. I don't even know who the judge is.

So, I'm a bit anxious.

However this isn't my first invitation to appear before a judge. I have another summons, "It is appointed for men to die once, and after that comes judgment."[10] But I don't feel the same anxiety about that appointment.

For I know what the judge will do. I know what the outcome will be. And most of all, I know who the judge is . . . he's my Father.

Chapter 12

Mouth-to-Mouth Manipulation

"Then the Pharisees left that place and made plans to trap Jesus in saying something wrong."

Matthew 22:15

In the coral reefs of the Caribbean lives a small fish known as the Kissing Fish. It's only about two to three inches long. It's bright blue and quick and a delight to behold. Most fascinating is its kiss. It's not uncommon to see two of these fish with lips pressed and fins thrashing. They give the appearance of serious underwater romance.

You would think the species would be an aquarium lover's dream. They look energetic, vivid, illuminant, and affectionate. But looks can be deceiving. For what appears to be a gentle friend in the sea is actually a pint-sized bully of the deep.

Ferociously territorial, the Kissing Fish has laid claim to its camp and wants no visitors. His square foot of coral is his and no one else's. He found it, he staked it out, and he wants no other of his kind near it.

Challenge his boundaries and he'll take you on, jaw to jaw. What appears to be a tryst is actually underwater martial arts.

Mouth pushing. Liplocking. Literal jawboning. Power moves with the tongue.

Sounds funny, doesn't it?

Sounds familiar, doesn't it?

We don't have to go to the Caribbean to see that type of power struggle. Mouth-to-mouth manipulation isn't limited to the Caribbean.

Look closely at the people in your world (or the person in your mirror). You might be surprised how fishy things get when people demand their way. Kissing Fish aren't the first to use their mouth to make their point.

In frontier days disputes were settled with quick fists; today we use a more sophisticated tool: the tongue. Just like the Kissing Fish we disguise our fights. We call it debating, challenging the status quo. In reality, it's nothing more than stubbornly defending our territory.

Such was the case on Tuesday during the last week in the life of Jesus. Long before the whips snapped, words were hurled. Long before the nails were hammered, accusations were made. Long before Jesus had to bear the cross, he had to bear the acid tongues of the religious leaders.

The dialogue appears innocent. No swords were drawn. No arrests were made. But don't let the apparent innocence fool you. Like the Kissing Fish the accusers were out for blood.

There were three encounters.

Case one: Show me your diploma please.

The procedure for being recognized as a religious teacher in Palestine was simple. Originally, rabbinical candidates had been ordained by a leading rabbi whom they respected and under whose teaching they served. This, however, led to variance in qualifications and teachings as well as widespread abuses. So the high Jewish council, the Sanhedrin, took over the responsibility for ordination.

At his ordination a man was declared to be a rabbi, elder, and judge and was given authority to teach, express wisdom, and render verdicts.

Fair procedure. Necessary safeguard. And so we aren't surprised that the religious leaders asked Jesus, "What authority do you have to do these things? Who gave you this authority?"[1] Had their questions stemmed from concern for the purity of the temple and the integrity of the position, there would have been no problem. But they wanted their territory: "We are afraid of what the crowd will do."[2]

Had they really cared about the future of the nation, they wouldn't have worried about what the people thought. They would have taken the matter of the rabbi into their own hands rather than worm away from him and eventually turn him over to a foreign government. They hadn't learned the first lesson of leadership. "A man who wants to lead the orchestra must turn his back on the crowd."

By the way, there is something odd in this picture. Do you see it? The created are asking the Creator about his credentials. The pot is asking the Potter for his I.D. No reference is made to the miracles. No question is raised about his teaching. They want to know about his ordination. Did he come out of the right seminary? Is he a member of the right denomination? Does he have the proper credentials?

Incredible. Cross-examining God. Now I see why powerful people often wear sunglasses—the spotlight blinds them to reality. They suffer from a delusion that power means something (it doesn't). They suffer from the misconception that titles make a difference (they don't). They are under the impression that earthly authority will make a heavenly difference (it won't).

Can I prove my point? Take this quiz.

Name the ten wealthiest men in the world.

Name the last ten Heisman trophy winners.

Name the last ten winners of the Miss America contest.

Name eight people who have won the Nobel or Pulitzer prize.

How about the last ten Academy Award winners for best picture or the last decade's worth of World Series winners?

How did you do? I didn't do well either. With the exception of you trivia hounds, none of us remember the headliners of yesterday too well. Surprising how quickly we forget, isn't it? And what I've mentioned above are no second-rate achievements. These are the best in their fields. But the applause dies. Awards tarnish. Achievements are forgotten. Accolades and certificates are buried with their owners.

Here's another quiz. See how you do on this one.

Think of three people you enjoy spending time with.

Name ten people who have taught you something worthwhile.

Name five friends who have helped you in a difficult time.

List a few teachers who have aided your journey through school.

Name half-a-dozen heroes whose stories have inspired you.

Easier? It was for me, too. The lesson? The people who make a difference are not the ones with the credentials, but the ones with the concern.

Case two: The sword in the studded scabbard.

"The Pharisees . . . made plans to trap Jesus in saying something wrong. . . . 'Teacher, we know that you are an honest man and that you teach the truth about God's way. You are not afraid of what other people think about you, because you pay no attention to who they are. So tell us what you think. Is it right to pay taxes to Caesar or not?' "[3]

Chances are that when a man slaps you on the back he wants you to cough up something. This is no exception. The Pharisees are doing some heavy backslapping in this verse. Though their question is valid, their motive is not. Of all the texts which drip with manipulation, this is the worst.

Like the Kissing Fish, the Pharisees appear gentle. But also like the Kissing Fish, something smells fishy.

God has made it clear that flattery is never to be a tool of the sincere servant. Flattery is nothing more than fancy dishonesty. It wasn't used by Jesus, nor should it be used by his followers.

"May the LORD cut off all flattering lips," affirmed the psalmist.[4]

"He who rebukes a man will in the end gain more favor than he who has a flattering tongue," agreed Solomon.[5]

"Beware of the man with sweet words and wicked deeds," learned Lucy.

The psalmist you've read. Solomon you've admired. But Lucy? She learned about flattery the hard way. Here's her story:

It's Washington, D.C., in the 1860s. The nation is ravaged by war. The country is divided with strife. But for young Lucy the greatest war is in her heart.

Lucy Lambert Hale was the younger daughter of John P. Hale, one of New Hampshire's Civil War senators. She was one of the most ravishing bachelorettes in our nation's capital. Her long list of suitors was testimony to her popularity. The list of those aspiring her heart was not only long, it was historical. More than one of her young loves grew to be national figures.

As early as the age of twelve she was receiving flowers from Will Chandler, a Harvard freshman. Lucy was fond of the young man but, after all, she was only twelve. Will became Secretary of the Navy and, eventually, a United States senator.

Then there was Oliver. Only two years her senior, he thought he had found his true love. She disagreed. Though he never got Lucy's hand, Oliver Wendell Holmes did get a seat on the Supreme Court.

But there was another man who, for a time, did occupy a place in her heart. And it is this man whose legacy in history is one of kind words and deadly deeds. His name was John.

While the war was raging in the nation, their love was raging in Washington. And while the nation was at odds, they, too, were often at odds. What confused Lucy about this most recent boyfriend was his inconsistency. He would state one thing and live another. His promises and performance didn't match. He would woo her with his words and bewilder her with his actions.

Consider this, the first letter he ever sent her, on Valentine's day, 1862.

> My Dear Miss Hale,
>
> Were it not for the License which a time-honored observance of this day allows, I had not written you this poor note.
>
> You resemble in a most remarkable degree a lady, very dear to me, now dead, and your close resemblance to her surprised me the first time I saw you. This must be my apology for any apparent rudeness noticeable—To see you has indeed afforded me a melancholy pleasure, if you can conceive of such and should we never meet nor I see you again—believe me, I shall always associate you in my memory, with her, who was very beautiful, and whose face, like your own I trust, was a faithful index of gentleness and amiability.
>
> With a thousand wishes for your future happiness I am, to you—
>
> > a Stranger

With words as sweet as molasses and determination as fierce as a bull, John made sure that he didn't remain too long a stranger. And with time, he and Lucy became engaged. That's when the war broke out—not in the country, but between John and Lucy.

He was insanely jealous. They quarreled incessantly. They argued as they listened to President Lincoln's second inaugural address. They quarreled the next night when John found Lucy dancing with the president's eldest son, Robert. They quarreled when the president appointed Lucy's father as ambassador to Spain. And John exploded when Lucy decided to break the engagement and go with her father to Spain.

John was kind with words, but possessive and jealous with actions. Lucy learned from John that a person can have words of honey and hands of steel. For that reason she left him. Ironically, she eventually married the man who had sent her flowers at the age of twelve, Will Chandler.

But though she lived a long and happy life, she would never forget the stormy romance with the man of kind words and harsh deeds. Nor would the rest of the world forget John Wilkes Booth.[6]

Now, I'm sure there was more to this story than a romance with a young girl, but for our case both the similarity and the lesson are significant. The words Jesus heard that day were just as kind. Who would have imagined they came from the lips of murderers? But therein lies the lesson of flattery. Treat it as cautiously as you would a jewel-embedded scabbard for within both are found a sword.

Case three: Myopic meanderings.

Enter: the Sadducees. "In this corner, weighing heavy on opinion and weak on balance, the aristocrats of Jerusalem, the Ivy Leaguers of Israel, the far left of the liberals—the Sadducees!"

This small band of leaders loved Greek philosophy and poo-pooed traditional Torah teaching as too rigid, too conservative. They were pro-Roman. The Pharisees were not—they were country club. The Sadducees were common—they thought there was no afterlife. The Pharisees could tell you what you were going to wear in the afterlife.

Normally, these two never would have been on the same side. But their fear of Jesus united them. The Sadducees made their money from the money-changing and dove-selling in the temple. Monday's temple cleansing convinced them they needed to send this fellow back to the sticks with his tail between his legs.

So, the Sadducees use the third trick of the tongue: hypothetical meandering. If this and that happens with this occurring before that . . . Their ploy is to create an extreme version of an unlikely incident and trap Jesus in his response.

If you want the long version of their question read Matthew 22:24-28. If you want the short version and my interpretation, here it is. "Teacher, Moses said if a married man dies without having children, his brother must marry the widow and have the children for him. Once there were seven brothers among us, blah, blah, blah, blah, blah . . ."

Just like the Kissing Fish, the Sadducees stubbornly protected tiny patches of territory. They, like the Kissing Fish, had limited vision. They battle over a little piece of ground. They fought over tiny territory in a great ocean.

There are those in the church who find a small territory and become obsessed with it. There are those in God's family who find a controversy and stake their claim to it. Every church has at least one stubborn soul who has mastered a minutiae of the message and made a mission out of it.

Myopic creatures fighting battles over needless turf.

Jesus' response is worth underlining. "You are way off." Now, your translation doesn't use those words and neither does mine. But it could. A fair translation of the Greek would be: "You are off-base. You are missing the point. You are chasing a rabbit down a dead-end trail."

Some time ago I came across a song by Dennis Tice which shows the absurdity of fighting over futile territory. With his permission, I share it with you. You'll love the title, it's called "Did Adam and Eve Have Navels?"

Did Adam and Eve have navels or a blank spot where it should be?
Do other folks lie awake at night or is it only me?
Thinkin' about the question that plagues all mankind
Hmmmmmmmmmm
Belly-button fuzz wuzza part of creation, how could I be so blind?
I think I'll start a church someday to preach this creed of mine
Cause Adam and Eve had navels and I'll prove it at the end of time.
Sure "God is love" and "Jesus saves," but what about this truth?
I found the answer just last year in 1st John chapter 2

Seek out the truth, the truth will set you free
Wait upon the Lord in all sincerity
And then you'll reach the highest level of Christianity
When you become a Navelist, your eyes will finally see
That Adam and Eve had navels, I'm telling you today
Yeah, I'm splitting hairs for Jesus and that makes it all okay
And I'm going to take you deeper than your eyes can currently see
I'm splittin' hairs for Jesus for more spirituality
I shared this truth with all the land and navelism grew
A thousand members growing strong, (cause I preach salvation too)
But now the church is splittin over some technicality,
Did their buttons go in or pop on out, how picky can they be?[7]

As long as Christians split hairs, Christians will split churches.

In his last week Jesus left a clear message: misuse of the mouth is noticed by God. The religious leaders thought they could manipulate Jesus with their words. They were wrong.

God is not trapped by trickery, flattered by flattery, or fooled by hypothesis. He wasn't then and isn't now.

The tragedy of the Kissing Fish is that he sees so little. All his oral warfare gets him is the same view from the same patch of coral. Had I a word with him, had I a moment with the creature who is possessed with a passion to protect his own and keep out what is new . . . I would challenge him to look around.

I would say what I need someone to say to me when I get territorial about my opinions: Let go of your territory for a while. Explore some new reefs. Scout some new regions. Much is gained by closing your mouth and opening your eyes.

Chapter 13

What Man Dared Not Dream

"What do you think about the Christ? Whose son is he?"
Matthew 22:42

Heroes mirror a society. Study a nation's heroes and understand the nation. We honor those who embody our dreams—gang members toast the ruthless, slaves esteem the freedom-fighter, and cult members exalt the dominant. The frail lionize the strong and the oppressed hallow the courageous.

The result is a collage of world heroes as opposite as Joseph Stalin is from Florence Nightingale, Peter Pan from George Patton, and Mark Twain from Mother Theresa. Each is an index to a chapter in the book called people.

One legendary character, however, reflects more than a culture—he reflects the globe. He is known the world over. A face as easily recognizable in Nigeria as in Indiana. One immortal whose story has been written by and told to people in every land.

If it is true that legends mirror a people, then this man is a mirror of the world. And we can learn much about ourselves by learning about him.

Some call him Sinterklaas. Others Pere Noel or Papa Noel. He's been known as Hoteiosho, Sonnerklaas, Father Christmas, Jelly Belly, and to most English speakers, Santa Claus.

His original name was Nicholas, which means victorious. He was born in A.D. 280 in what is now Turkey. He was orphaned at age nine when his parents died of a plague. Though many would think Santa majored in toy-making and minored in marketing, actually the original Nicholas studied Greek philosophy and Christian doctrine.

He was honored by the Catholic church by being named Bishop of Myra in the early fourth century. He held the post until his death on December 6, 343.

History recognized him as a saint, but in the third century he was a bit of a troublemaker. He was twice jailed, once by the Emperor Diocletian for religious reasons, the other for slugging a fellow bishop during a fiery debate. (So much for finding out who is naughty and nice.)

Old Nick never married. But that's not to say he wasn't a romantic. He was best known for the kindness he showed to a poor neighbor who was unable to support his three daughters or provide the customary dowry so they could attract husbands. Old Saint Nicholas slipped up to the house by night and dropped a handful of gold coins through the window so the eldest daughter could afford to get married. He repeated this act on two other nights for the other two daughters.

This story was the seed which, watered with years, became the Santa legend. It seems that every generation adorned it with another ornament until it sparkled more than a Christmas tree.

The gift grew from a handful of coins to bags of coins. Instead of dropping them through the window, he dropped them down the chimney. And rather than land on the floor, the bags of coins landed in the girls' stockings which were hanging on the hearth to dry. (So that's where all this stocking stuff started.)

The centuries have been as good to Nicholas's image as to his deeds. Not only have his acts been embellished, his wardrobe and personality have undergone transformations as well.

As Bishop of Myra he wore the traditional ecclesiastical robes and a mitered hat. He is known to have been slim, with a dark beard and a serious personality.

By 1300 he was wearing a white beard. By the 1800s he was depicted with a rotund belly and an ever-present basket of food over his arm. Soon came the black boots, a red cape, and a cheery stocking on his head. In the late nineteenth century his basket of food became a sack of toys. In 1866 he was small and gnomish but by 1930 he was a robust six-footer with rosy cheeks and a Coca-Cola.

Santa reflects the desires of people all over the world. With the centuries he had become the composite of what we want:

A friend who cares enough to travel a long way against all odds to bring good gifts to good people.

A sage who, though aware of each act, has a way of rewarding the good and overlooking the bad.

A friend of children who never gets sick and never grows old.

A father who lets you sit on his lap and share your deepest desires.

Santa. The culmination of what we need in a hero. The personification of our passions. The expression of our yearnings. The fulfillment of our desires.

And . . . the betrayal of our meager expectations.

What? you say. Let me explain.

You see, Santa can't provide what we really need. For one thing, he's only around once a year. When January winds chill our souls he's history. When December's requests become February payments, Santa's left the mall. When April demands taxes or May brings final exams, Santa is still months from his next visit. And should July find us ill or October find us alone we can't go to his chair for comfort—it's still empty. He only comes once a year.

And when he comes, though he gives much, he doesn't take away much. He doesn't take away the riddle of the grave, the burden of mistakes, or the anxiety of demands. He's kind and quick and cute; but when it comes to healing hurts—don't go to Santa.

Now, I don't mean to be a Scrooge. I'm not wanting to slam the jolly old fellow. I am just pointing out that we people are timid when it comes to designing legends.

You'd think we could do better. You'd think that over six centuries we'd develop a hero who'd resolve those fears.

But we can't. We have made many heroes, from King Arthur to Kennedy; Lincoln to Lindbergh; Socrates to Santa to Superman. We give it the best we can, every benefit of every doubt, every supernatural strength, and, for a brief shining moment we have the hero we need—the king who can deliver Camelot. But then the truth leaks and fact surfaces amidst the fiction and the chinks in the armor are seen. And we realize that the heroes, as noble as they may have been, as courageous as they were, were conceived in the same stained society as you and I.

Except one. There was one who claimed to come from a different place. There was one who, though he had the appearance of a man, claimed to have the origin of God. There was one who, while wearing the face of a Jew, had the image of the Creator.

Those who saw him—really saw him—knew there was something different. At his touch blind beggars saw. At his command crippled legs walked. At his embrace empty lives filled with vision.

He fed a thousand with one basket. He stilled a storm with one command. He raised the dead with one proclamation. He changed lives with one request. He rerouted the history of the world with one life, lived in one country, was born in one manger, and died on one hill.

During his final week he summarized his claims with one question. Speaking of himself he asked his disciples, "What do you think about the Christ? Whose son is he?"[1]

A probing question. A properly positioned question. The "what" is answered by the "who." What you think about the Christ is embosomed in whose son he is. Note Jesus didn't ask, "What do you think about the Christ and his teachings?" or, "What do you think about the Christ and his opinions on social issues?" or, "What do you think about the Christ and his ability to lead people?"

After three years of ministry, hundreds of miles, thousands of miracles, innumerable teachings, Jesus asks, "Who?" Jesus bids the people to ponder not what he has done but who he is.

It's the ultimate question of the Christ: Whose son is he?

Is he the son of God or the sum of our dreams? Is he the force of creation or a figment of our imagination?

When we ask that question about Santa, the answer is the culmination of our desires. A depiction of our fondest dreams.

Not so when we ask it about Jesus. For no one could ever dream a person as incredible as he is. The idea that a virgin would be selected by God to bear himself.... The notion that God would don a scalp and toes and two eyes.... The thought that the King of the universe would sneeze and burp and get bit by mosquitoes.... It's too incredible. Too revolutionary. We would never create such a Savior. We aren't that daring.

When we create a redeemer, we keep him safely distant in his faraway castle. We allow him only the briefest of encounters with us. We permit him to swoop in and out with his sleigh before we can draw too near. We wouldn't ask him to take up residence in the midst of a contaminated people. In our wildest imaginings we wouldn't conjure a king who becomes one of us.

But God did. God did what we wouldn't dare dream. He did what we couldn't imagine. He became a man so we could trust him. He became a sacrifice so we could know him. And he defeated death so we could follow him.

It defies logic. It is a divine insanity. A holy incredibility. Only a God beyond systems and common sense could create a plan as absurd as this. Yet, it is the very impossibility of it all that makes it possible. The wildness of the story is its strongest witness.

For only a God could create a plan this mad. Only a Creator beyond the fence of logic could offer such a gift of love.

What man can't do, God does.

So, when it comes to goodies and candy, cherub cheeks and red noses, go to the North Pole.

But when it comes to eternity, forgiveness, purpose, and truth, go to the manger. Kneel with the shepherds. Worship the God who dared to do what man dared not dream.

Chapter 14

The Cursor or the Cross?

"How are you going to escape God's judgment?"
Matthew 23:33

What I don't like about computers is that they do what I say and not what I mean.

Example: I mean to hit the "control" button but hit the "CAPS LOCK" BUTTON AND ALL OF A SUDDEN GIANT LETTERS DOMINATE THE SCREEN. i LOOK AT THE SCREEN AND SAY, "tHAT'S NOT WHAT i MEANT!" AND i correct my mistake.

Here's another example.

I want to correct one letter but inadvertently hit the button that removes the entire   . "That's not what I meant," I mumble to the one-eyed monster, and then I correct my mistake.

Now I know I shouldn't be so hard on the mACHINE (OOPS, DID IT AGAIN). After all, it's just a tool. It can't read my mind (though considering what it cost, it should at least keep me from making the same mistake over and over). A computer computes. It doesn't think. It doesn't question. It doesn't smile, shake its monitor, and say, "Max, Max, I know what you are trying to do. You don't intend to be hitting the delete button, removing the very letters you want to keep. If you'd look at your screen you would see that. But since you won't and since you and I are good friends and you leave me plugged in, I'm going to give you what you need and not what you request."

Computers don't do that. Computers are legalists, impersonal pragmatists. Push a button and get a response. Learn the system and get the printout. Blow the system and get ready for a long night.

Computers are heartless creatures. Don't expect any compassion from your lap top. They don't call it a hard disk for nothing. (Even the shell is hard.)

Some folks have a computer theology when it comes to understanding God. God is the ultimate desktop. The Bible is the maintenance manual, the Holy Spirit is the floppy disk, and Jesus is the 1-800 service number.

Call it computerized Christianity. Push the right buttons, enter the right code, insert the correct data, and bingo, print out your own salvation.

It's professional religion. You do your part and the Divine Computer does his. No need to pray (after all, you control the keyboard). No emotional attachment necessary (who wants to hug circuits?). And worship? Well, worship is a lab exercise—insert the rituals and see the results.

Computerized religion. No kneeling. No weeping. No gratitude. No emotion. It's great—unless you make a mistake. Unless you err. Unless you enter the wrong data or forget to save the manuscript. Unless you're caught on the wrong side of a power surge. And then . . . tough luck, buddy, you're on your own.

Religion by computer. That's what happens when . . .

you replace the living God with a cold system;

you replace inestimable love with pro-forma budget;

you replace the ultimate sacrifice of Christ with the puny achievements of man.

When you view God as a computer and the Christian as a number-crunching, cursor-commanding, button-pusher . . . that is religion by the computer.

God hates it. It crushes his people. It contaminates his leaders. It corrupts his children.

How do I know? He said so. Jesus condemns religion by the rules. With eyes blazing and pistols firing, Jesus rips hole after hole in the hot-air balloon of the Pharisees. His sermon on Tuesday is a one-sided shootout. The result is a permanent proclamation of God against systematic salvation.

Let me see if a simple exercise will clarify this point. How would you fill in this blank?

A person is made right with God through _____.

Simple statement. Yet don't let its brevity fool you. How you complete it is critical; it reflects the nature of your faith.

A person is made right with God through . . .

Being good. A person is made right with God through goodness. Pay your taxes. Give sandwiches to the poor. Don't drive too fast or drink too much or drink at all. Christian conduct—that's the secret.

Suffering. There's the answer. That's how to be made right with God—suffer. Sleep on dirt floors. Stalk through dank jungles. Malaria. Poverty. Cold days. Night-long vigils. Vows of chastity. Shaved heads, bare feet. The greater the pain, the greater the saint.

No, no, no. The way to be made right with God? Doctrine. Dead-center interpretation of the truth. Air-tight theology which explains every mystery. The Millennium simplified. Inspiration clarified. The role of women defined once and for all. God has to save us—we know more than he does.

How are we made right with God? All of the above are tried. All are taught. All are demonstrated. But none are from God.

In fact, that is the problem. None are from God. All are from people. Think about it. Who is the major force in the above examples? Humankind or God? Who does the saving, you or him?

If we are saved by good works, we don't need God—weekly reminders of the do's and don'ts will get us to heaven. If we are saved by suffering, we certainly don't need God. All we need is a whip and a chain and the gospel of guilt. If we are saved by doctrine then, for heaven's sake, let's study! We don't need God, we need a lexicon. Weigh the issues. Explore the options. Decipher the truth.

But be careful, student. For if you are saved by having exact doctrine, then one mistake would be fatal. That goes for those who believe we are made right with God through deeds. I hope the temptation is never greater than the strength. If it is, a bad fall could be a bad omen. And those who think we are saved by suffering, take caution as well, for you never know how much suffering is required.

In fact, if you are saving yourself, you never know for sure about anything. You never know if you've hurt enough, wept enough, or learned enough. Such is the result of computerized religion: fear, insecurity, instability. And, most ironically, arrogance.

That's right—arrogance. The insecure boast the most. Those who are trying to save themselves promote themselves. Those saved by works display works. Those saved by suffering unveil scars. Those saved by emotion flash their feelings. And those saved by doctrine—you got it. They wear their doctrine on their sleeves.

Or, as was the case of the Pharisees, on their head: "They make the boxes of Scriptures that they wear bigger."[1]

Or on their shoulders: "They make their special prayer clothes very long."[2]

Or they demand the choice seats: They "love to have the most important seats at feasts and in the synagogues."[3]

And they take great pride in titles. "They love people to greet them with respect in the marketplaces, and they love to have people call them 'Teacher.' "[4]

The Pharisees were arrogant. They were arrogant because they were self-righteous. They were self-righteous because they were trying to make themselves righteous without God. They had turned the temple into a computer network. The synagogue was a programming course, the rituals were the keyboard, and the Pharisees were the programmers. They were the authorities. They were right and they knew it.

"They do good things so that other people will see them."[5]

It made Jesus furious. So furious that his last sermon for the Pharisees was not about love or compassion or evangelism. It was about phony faith and hollow hearts. It was an in-your-face slam dunk against legalistic leadership.

Six times he called them hypocrites and five times he called them blind. He accused them of kamikaze fatalism—choosing hell over heaven and taking everybody with them. Instead of converting people to God they made clones of themselves. They complicated the gospel with odd myths and superstition. They took pride when it came to tithing, but took naps when it came to serving.[6]

Their faith was as appealing as eating out of a bowl crusty with yesterday's lentil or as aromatic as digging up last century's graves. They were about as innocent as Freddie Kruger and as sincere as a pimp.

"You are snakes," Jesus accused, seeing in their eyes the same beady blackness which Eve had seen in the garden.

What angered Jesus during his last week was not the apostles' confusion. He wasn't upset by the people's demands. He didn't lose his temper with the soldiers and their whips nor explode with Pilate and his questions. But the one thing he could not stomach was two-faced faith: Religion used for profit and religion used for prestige. This he could not tolerate.

Thirty-six verses of fire were summarized with one question: "How are you going to escape God's judgment?"[7]

Good question. Good question for the Pharisees, good question for you and me. How are we going to escape God's judgment?

That question is answered by going back to the blank and filling it in. A person is made right with God through _____.

Ironically, or appropriately, it was a Pharisee who first wrote that line. Or, at least, he used to be a Pharisee. He got his training in front of a theological terminal. He was an up-and-coming religious technician. He could answer the pickiest questions and solve the most minute riddle. But, the big question, Jesus' question, he couldn't answer.

I wonder if he was present the day Jesus asked it? "How will you escape God's judgment?" Maybe he was. Maybe his young face was in the crowd. Perhaps he was there, scrolls under the arm, scowl on the face. Heir-apparent to the legalistic swivel chair.

I wonder if he was there. . . .

If he was, he had no answer. No legalist does. The man who would save himself says nothing in God's presence. All of a sudden, our best efforts are pitifully puny. Dare you stand before God and ask him to save you because of your suffering or your sacrifice or your tears or your study?

Nor do I.

Nor did Paul. It took him decades to discover what he wrote in only one sentence.

"A person is made right with God through faith."[8] Not through good works, suffering, or study. All those may be the result of salvation but they are not the cause of it.

How will you escape God's judgment? Only one way. Through faith in God's sacrifice. It's not what you do, it's what he did.

ᘛᘚ

By the way, my computer still drives me crazy. It still does WHAT i SAY, OOps, and not what I mean. I push the wrong button, I pay the price. For that reason, I refuse to call it what the manufacturer does. It is not a personal computer. It is cold, detached, and could care less about my happiness.

A personal computer would be different. In fact it wouldn't be a computer at all, it would be a friend. A friend who gives me what I need instead of what I request. A friend who knows more about me than I do. A friend who doesn't have to be turned off at night and on in the morning.

A computer like that? Too much to ask, I know.

A God like that? Still too much to ask. But that's what he is. Why else do you think he is known as your personal Savior?

Chapter 15

Unclutterred
Faith

> *"So do not let anyone make rules for you."*
> Colossians 2:16

*B*edtime is a bad time for kids. No child understands the logic of going to bed while there is energy left in the body or hours left in the day.

My children are no exception. A few nights ago, after many objections and countless groans, the girls were finally in their gowns, in their beds, and on their pillows. I slipped into the room to give them a final kiss. Andrea, the five-year-old was still awake, just barely, but awake. After I kissed her, she lifted her eyelids one final time and said, "I can't wait until I wake up."

Oh, for the attitude of a five-year-old! That simple uncluttered passion for living that can't wait for tomorrow. A philosophy of life that reads, "Play hard, laugh hard, and leave the worries to your father." A bottomless well of optimism flooded by a perpetual spring of faith. Is it any wonder Jesus said we must have the heart of a child before we can enter the kingdom of heaven?

I like the way J. B. Phillips renders Jesus' call to childlikeness: "Jesus called a little child to his side and set him on his feet in the middle of them all. 'Believe me,' he said, 'unless you change your whole outlook and become like little children you will never enter the kingdom of Heaven.' "[1]

Note the phrase "change your whole outlook." No small command. Quit looking at life like an adult and see it through the eyes of a child.

Essential counsel for us sober-minded, serious-faced, sour-pussed adults. Necessary advice for we Charles Atlas wannabes who shoulder the world. Good words for those of us who seldom say, "I can't wait until I wake up," and more often state, "I can't wait to go to bed."

We are like children in one way. We groan about bed just like they do—only we groan about getting out of it instead of getting into it.

It's not hard to understand why.

Who gets excited about climbing into the world many wake up to? Deadlines upon traffic jams upon grumpy bosses and crowded streets. Keeping your head to the pillow is much more appealing than keeping your shoulder to the wheel.

One word summarizes the frustration of most people— confusion. Nothing seems simple. Have you attempted to understand mortgage options lately? Tried to understand the moods of your mate? Bought a new phone system for your office recently? Tried to fix a microwave or decipher a therapist's counsel? Then you know what I mean.

Enter, religion. We Christians have a solution for the confusion don't we? "Leave the cluttered world of humanity," we invite, "and enter the sane, safe garden of religion."

Let's be honest. Instead of a "sane, safe garden," how about a "wild and woolly sideshow"? It shouldn't be the case, but when you step back and look at how religion must appear to the unreligious, well, the picture of an amusement park comes to mind.

Flashing lights of ceremony and pomp. Roller-coaster thrills of emotion. Loud music. Strange people. Funny clothes.

Like barkers on a midway preachers persuade: "Step right up to the Church of Heavenly Hope of High Angels and Happy Hearts. . . ."

"Over here, Madam, that church is too tough on folks like you. Try us, we teach salvation by sanctification which leads to purification and stabilization. That is unless you prefer the track of predestination which offers . . ."

"Your attention, please sir. Try our premillennial, noncharismatic, Calvinistic Creed service on for size . . . you won't be disappointed."

A safe garden of serenity? No wonder a lady said to me once, "I'd like to try Jesus, if I could just get past the religion."

She speaks for thousands. She may speak for you. Perhaps you long to wake up to the same life my daughter does: playful, peaceful, and secure. You haven't found it in the world and you've peeked in the church doors and aren't too sure about what you see there either.

Or maybe you've done more than peek through the church doors, you've gone in and gotten to work. You've baked, visited, volunteered, and taught. But instead of rest you got stress. And now you are puzzled because Jesus said you should feel at peace and since you don't, it certainly must be your fault. God wouldn't say that and not do it, would he? So in addition to being confused by the world and the church you are confused at your own inability to make sense out of it all.

Whew! Being a Christian is hard work!

It's not supposed to be though. Complicated religion wasn't made by God. Reading Matthew 23 will convince you of that. It is the crackdown of Christ on midway religion.

If you've always thought of Jesus as a pale-faced, milquetoast Tiny Tim, then read this chapter and see the other side: an angry father denouncing the pimps who have prostituted his children.

Six times he calls them hypocrites. Five times he calls them blind. Seven times he denounces them and once he prophesies their ruin. Not what you would call a public relations presentation.

But in the midst of the roaring river of words there is a safe island of instruction. Somewhere between bursts of fire Jesus holsters his pistol, turns to the wide-eyed disciples, and describes the essence of simple faith. Four verses: a reading as brief as it is practical. Call it Christ's solution to complicated Christianity.

"You must not be called 'Teacher,' because you have only one Teacher, and you are all brothers and sisters together. And don't call any person on earth 'Father,' because you have one Father, who is in heaven. And you should not be called 'Master,' because you have only one Master, the Christ. Whoever is your servant is the greatest among you. Whoever makes himself great will be made humble. Whoever makes himself humble will be made great."[2]

How do you simplify your faith? How do you get rid of the clutter? How do you discover a joy worth waking up to? Simple. Get rid of the middleman.

Discover truth for yourself. "You have only one Teacher, and you are all brothers and sisters together."[3]

Develop trust for yourself. "Don't call any person on earth 'Father,' because you have one Father, who is in heaven."[4]

Discern his will for yourself. "You have only one Master, the Christ."[5]

There are some who position themselves between you and God. There are some who suggest the only way to get to God is through them. There is the great teacher who has the final word on Bible teaching. There is the father who must bless your acts. There is the spiritual master who will tell you what God wants you to do. Jesus' message for complicated religion is to remove these middlemen.

He's not saying that you don't need teachers, elders, or counselors. He is saying, however, that we are all brothers and sisters and have equal access to the Father. Simplify your faith by seeking God for yourself. No confusing ceremonies necessary. No mysterious rituals required. No elaborate channels of command or levels of access.

You have a Bible? You can study. You have a heart? You can pray. You have a mind? You can think.

One of my favorite stories concerns a bishop who was traveling by ship to visit a church across the ocean. While en route, the ship stopped at an island for a day. He went for a walk on a beach. He came upon three fishermen mending their nets.

Curious about their trade he asked them some questions. Curious about his ecclesiastical robes, they asked him some questions. When they found out he was a Christian leader, they got excited. "We Christians!" they said, proudly pointing to one another.

The bishop was impressed but cautious. Did they know the Lord's Prayer? They had never heard of it.

"What do you say, then, when you pray?"

"We pray, 'We are three, you are three, have mercy on us.' "

The bishop was appalled at the primitive nature of the prayer. "That will not do." So he spent the day teaching them the Lord's Prayer. The fishermen were poor but willing learners. And before the bishop sailed away the next day, they could recite the prayer with no mistakes.

The bishop was proud.

On the return trip the bishop's ship drew near the island again. When the island came into view the bishop came to the deck and recalled with pleasure the men he had taught and resolved to go see them again. As he was thinking a light appeared on the horizon near the island. It seemed to be getting nearer. As the bishop gazed in wonder he realized the three fishermen were walking toward him on the water. Soon all the passengers and crew were on the deck to see the sight.

When they were within speaking distance, the fisherman cried out, "Bishop, we come hurry to meet you."

"What is it you want?" asked the stunned bishop.

"We are so sorry. We forget lovely prayer. We say, 'Our Father, who art in heaven, hallowed be your name . . .' and then we forget.

Please tell us prayer again."

The bishop was humbled. "Go back to your homes, my friends, and when you pray say, 'We are three, you are three, have mercy on us.'"

Seek the simple faith. Major in the majors. Focus on the critical. Long for God.

"I can't wait to wake up," are the words of a child's faith. The reason Andrea can say them is because her world is simple. She plays hard, she laughs much, and she leaves the worries to her father.

Let's do the same.

Chapter 16

Surviving Life

"But those people who keep their faith until the end will be saved. The Good News about God's kingdom will be preached in all the world, to every nation. Then the end will come."

Matthew 24:13-14

Not all of you will understand this chapter. Not all of you will comprehend its message or relate to its promise. You won't understand it if:

You've never failed and are intolerant of those who have.

Your life is as hygienic as a new hospital and your soul could pass the white glove test.

You are a red-hot zealot who thinks God is lucky to have you on his side.

You dreamed of a perfect home and got it; dreamed of the perfect job and got it; dreamed of the problem-free life and got it.

Your pillow has never known tears, your prayers have never known anguish, and your faith has never known doubt.

If you are tearless and fearless and can't understand why others aren't, then this chapter is going to sound like a foreign language.

Why? Because this is a chapter on survival. The next few pages deal with coping with pain. The following paragraphs were not written for those on top of the world, but for those trapped under one which has collapsed. If you can relate to that description, then turn to Matthew and get ready for some assurance.

That may surprise you if you know anything about Matthew 24. You remember it as the neighborhood hangout for end-times fanatics. The camping ground for eschatological mathematicians and last-days prophets.

It deserves that reputation. This section known as the Olivet discourse is Christ's proclamation of the end times. Scholars have dedicated more than one book to this one chapter to answer one question: What is Jesus saying?

Ominous phrases lurk in the chapter: "wars and rumors of wars," "the destroying terror," and "how terrible it will be for women who are pregnant." Eerie descriptions of the sun growing dark and the moon not giving its light. Vultures hovering around bodies and lightning flashing.

How do we explain it?

Some feel the entire chapter is symbolic and mustn't be interpreted literally. Others feel it is a combination of comments equally applied to the destruction of Jerusalem and the return of Christ. Still others state that the chapter has one purpose and that is to prepare us for the final judgment.

We know two things for sure. First, Jesus is preparing his disciples for a cataclysmic future. His words of disaster rang true in A.D. 70 when Jerusalem was brought to her knees by the Romans. His words will ring true again when he comes to reclaim his own and put a period after history.

We also know, however, that cataclysms don't just occur in Jerusalem and at the end of history. Hungry bodies and cold hearts are easily found today. The counsel Jesus gives on surviving tough times is useful for more than the battles of Rome and Armageddon. It is useful for the battles of your world and mine.

So, if you are looking for my prediction of the day Christ will return, sorry. You won't find it here. He hasn't chosen to give us that date, so time spent speculating is time poorly used.

He has chosen, however, to give a manual of survival for lives under siege.

"As Jesus left the Temple and was walking away, his followers came up to him to show him the Temple's buildings. Jesus asked, 'Do you see all these buildings? I tell you the truth, not one stone will be left on another. Every stone will be thrown down to the ground." [1]

It's impossible to overstate the role of the temple in the Jewish mind. The temple was the meeting place between God and man. It represented the atonement, the sacrifice, and the priesthood. It was the structure that represented the heart of the people.

The temple was dazzling; built with white marble and plated with gold. In the sun it shone so bright as to test the eyes. The temple area was surrounded by porches and on these porches were pillars cut out of solid marble in one piece. They were thirty-seven-and-a-half feet high and so thick that three men joining hands could barely encircle one. Archaeologists have found cornerstones from the temple which measure twenty to forty feet in length and weigh more than four hundred tons. [2]

What an impressive sight this must have been for the rural followers of Jesus! Little wonder they were slack-jawed. But more stirring than what they saw was what they heard Jesus say, "I tell you the truth, not one stone will be left on another. Every stone will be thrown down to the ground."

There is pathos in the simple phrase which begins the chapter, "He was walking away from it." Jesus has turned his back on the temple. [3] The one who called for the construction of the temple is walking away from it. The Holy One has abandoned the cherished mountain.

He told them, "The whole thing will come crashing down." [4]

To say the temple would crash was to say the nation would crash. The temple was the people. For over a millennium the temple had been the heart of Israel and now Jesus was saying the heart would break. "Your house will be left completely empty,"⁵ he told the Pharisees earlier in the day.

And crash it did. In A.D. 70, Titus, the Roman general, laid siege to the city. Being set on a hill, Jerusalem was difficult to take. So Titus resolved to starve it. The grim horror of the famine is a black day in Jewish history. Let the historian Josephus describe the siege:

> Then did the famine widen in its progress, and devoured people by whole houses and families; the upper rooms were full of women and children that were dying of famine; and the lanes of the city were full of dead bodies of the aged; the children also and young men wandered about the marketplaces like shadows, all swelled with famine and fell down dead wheresoever their misery seized them. . . . The famine confounded all natural passions; for those who were just going to die looked upon those who were gone to their rest before them with dry eyes and open mouths. A deep silence, also, and a kind of deadly night had seized upon the city . . . and every one of them died with their eyes fixed upon the Temple.⁶

A holocaust: 97,000 were taken captive and 1,100,000 were slain. It was this disaster that Jesus foresaw. It was for this disaster that he prepared his disciples. And it is this type of disaster that can strike your world.

Some years ago we took a family vacation to Santa Fe, New Mexico. Denalyn and I decided to be adventurous and ride the rapids of the Rio Grande. We drove to the designated spot and there met the guide and the other courageous tourists.

His instructions were foreboding.

"When you fall in the water . . ." he began.

"And when you find yourself floating in the river . . ."

"And when the boat flips over . . ." I was beginning to get nervous, I elbowed Denalyn and whispered, "Notice he doesn't say 'if'."

Nor did Jesus. Jesus didn't say, "In this world you may have trouble" or, "In this world there are some who have trouble." No, he assured us, "In this world you will have trouble."[7] If you have a pulse you will have pain. If you are a person you will have problems.

In Matthew 24 Jesus prepares his disciples by telling them what will happen.

"Many will come in my name, saying, 'I am the Christ,' and they will fool many people."[8]

"You will hear about wars and stories of wars that are coming, but don't be afraid. These things must happen before the end comes."[9]

"There will be times when there is no food for people to eat, and there will be earthquakes in different places. These things are like the first pains when something new is about to be born."[10]

"Then people will arrest you, hand you over to be hurt, and kill you. They will hate you because you believe in me."[11]

Far from a pep rally don't you think? More like a last word given by an officer before the soldiers go to battle. More like a lesson Charles Hall would give his demolition team.

Charles Hall blows up bombs for a living. He is a part of the EOD—the Explosive Ordinance Demolition. He is paid $1,500 a week to walk the sands of post-war Kuwait searching for live mines or discarded grenades.

Richard Lowther, another EOD expert, has spent years blowing up some of the thousands of sea mines left over from World Wars I and II. He said, "Every time I pick up the paper and read about a new civil war I think 'Great, as soon as it's over I'll be there.' "[12]

You and I and these EODs have a lot in common: treacherous trails through explosive territories. Problems which lay partly obscured by the sand. A constant threat of losing life or limb.

And most significant, we, like the demolition team, are called to walk through a mine field which we didn't create. Such is the case with many of life's struggles. We didn't create them, but we have to live with them.

We didn't make alcohol, but our highways have drunk drivers. We don't sell drugs, but our neighborhoods have those who do. We didn't create international tension, but we have to fear the terrorists. We didn't train the thieves, but each of us is a potential victim of their greed.

We, like the EODs, are tiptoeing through a mine field which we didn't create.

The disciples were about to do the same. The collapse of the temple wasn't their fault; they weren't to be blamed for the rejection of Christ. It wasn't because of them that Jesus said the "house will be left completely empty," but because they lived in a sinful world they would be victims of sin's consequences.

If you live on a shooting range chances are you are going to catch a bullet. If you live on a battlefield a cannon ball will likely land in your yard. If you walk through a dark room, you may stub your toe. If you walk through a mine field you may lose your life.

And if you live in a world darkened by sin, you may be its victim.

Jesus is honest about the life we are called to lead. There is no guarantee that just because we belong to him we will go unscathed. No promise is found in Scripture that says when you follow the king you are exempt from battle. No, often just the opposite is the case.

How do we survive the battle? How do we endure the fray?

Jesus gives three certainties. Three assurances. Three absolutes. Imagine him leaning closer and looking deeply into the wide eyes of the disciples. Knowing the jungle they are about to enter he gives them three compasses which, if used, will keep them on the right trail.

First, assurance of victory: "Those people who keep their faith until the end will be saved."[13]

He doesn't say if you succeed you will be saved. Or if you come out on top you will be saved. He says if you endure. An accurate rendering would be, "If you hang in there until the end . . . if you go the distance."

The Brazilians have a great phrase for this. In Portuguese, a person who has the ability to hang in and not give up has *garra*. *Garra* means "claws." What imagery! A person with *garra* has claws which burrow into the side of the cliff and keep him from falling.

So do the saved. They may get close to the edge, they may even stumble and slide. But they will dig their nails into the rock of God and hang on.

I've been told that during the filming of *Ben Hur*, Charleton Heston had trouble learning to drive a chariot (who wouldn't?). With much practice he was finally able to control the vehicle, but still had some doubts. He reportedly explained his concerns to the director Cecil B. DeMille by saying, "I think I can drive the chariot, but I'm not sure I can win the race."

DeMille responded, "You just stay in the race and I'll make sure you win."

Jesus gives you the same assurance. You stay in the race, he'll make sure you get home. Those who have *garra* will be saved.

Secondly, Jesus gives the assurance of accomplishment: "The Good News about God's kingdom will be preached in all the world, to every nation."[14]

In 1066 one of the most decisive battles in the history of the world was fought. William, Duke of Normandy, dared to invade England. The English were a formidable opponent anywhere, but next to invincible in their own land.

But William had something the English did not. He had invented a device which gave his army a heavy advantage in battle. He had an edge: the stirrup.

Conventional wisdom of the day was that a horse was too unstable a platform from which to fight. As a result soldiers would ride their horses to the battlefield and then dismount before engaging in combat. But the Norman army, standing secure in their stirrups, were able to ride down the English. They were faster and they were stronger.

The stirrup led to the conquest of England. Without it, William might never have challenged such an enemy. And this book might have been written in Old English.

Because they had a way to stand in the battle, they were victorious after the battle. Jesus' assurance of victory was daring. Look at his listeners: upcountry fishermen and laborers whose eyes bug at the sight of a big city. You'd have been hard-pressed to find anyone who would wage that the prophecy would come to pass.

But it did, just fifty-three days later. Fifty-three days later Jews were in Jerusalem from "every country in the world."[15] Peter stood before them and told them about Jesus.

The disciples were emboldened with the assurance that the task would be completed. Because they had a way to stand in the battle, they were victorious after the battle. They had an edge . . . and so do we.

Lastly, Jesus gives us assurance of completion: "Then the end will come."[16]

An intriguing verse is found in 1 Thessalonians 4:16, "The Lord himself will come down from heaven with a loud command."

Have you ever wondered what that command will be? It will be the inaugural word of heaven. It will be the first audible message most have heard from God. It will be the word which closes one age and opens a new one.

I think I know what the command will be. I could very well be wrong, but I think the command which puts an end to the pains of the earth and initiates the joys of heaven will be two words:

"No more."

The King of kings will raise his pierced hand and proclaim, "No more."

The angels will stand and the Father will speak, "No more."

Every person who lives and who ever lived will turn toward the sky and hear God announce, "No more."

No more loneliness.

No more tears.

No more death. No more sadness. No more crying. No more pain.

As John sat on the Island of Patmos surrounded by sea and separated from friends he dreamt of the day when God would say, "No more."

This same disciple who had heard Jesus speak these words of assurance over a half a century before now knew what they meant. I wonder if he could hear the voice of Jesus in his memory.

"The end will come."

For those who live for this world, that's bad news. But for those who live for the world to come, it's an encouraging promise.

You're in a land mine, my friend, and it's only a matter of time: "For in this world you will have trouble. . . ." Next time you are tossed into a river as you ride the rapids of life, remember his words of assurance.

Those who endure will be saved.

The gospel will be preached.

The end will come.

You can count on it.

Chapter 17

Sandcastle Stories

"They knew nothing about what was happening."
Matthew 24:39

Hot sun. Salty air. Rhythmic waves.

A little boy is on the beach. On his knees he scoops and packs the sand with plastic shovels into a bright red bucket. Then he upends the bucket on the surface and lifts it. And, to the delight of the little architect, a castle tower is created.

All afternoon he will work. Spooning out the moat. Packing the walls. Bottle tops will be sentries. Popsicle sticks will be bridges. A sandcastle will be built.

❧

Big city. Busy streets. Rumbling traffic.

A man is in his office. At his desk he shuffles papers into stacks and delegates assignments. He cradles the phone on his shoulder and punches the keyboard with his fingers. Numbers are juggled and contracts are signed and much to the delight of the man, a profit is made.

All his life he will work. Formulating the plans. Forecasting the future. Annuities will be sentries. Capital gains will be bridges. An empire will be built.

Two builders of two castles. They have much in common. They shape granules into grandeurs. They see nothing and make something. They are diligent and determined. And for both the tide will rise and the end will come.

Yet, that is where the similarities cease. For the boy sees the end while the man ignores it. Watch the boy as the dusk approaches. Each wave slaps an inch closer to his creation. Every crest crashes closer than the one before.

But the boy doesn't panic. He is not surprised. All day the pounding waves have reminded him that the end is inevitable. He knows the secret of the surging. Soon they will come and take his castle into the deep.

The man, however, doesn't know the secret. He should. He, like the boy, lives surrounded by rhythmic reminders. Days come and go. Seasons ebb and flow. Every sunrise which becomes a sunset whispers the secret, "Time will take your castles."

So, one is prepared and one isn't. One is peaceful while the other panics.

As the waves near, the wise child jumps to his feet and begins to clap. There is no sorrow. No fear. No regret. He knew this would happen. He is not surprised. And when the great breaker crashes into his castle and his masterpiece is sucked into the sea, he smiles.

He smiles, picks up his tools, takes his father's hand, and goes home.

The grown-up, however, is not so wise. As the wave of years collapses on his castle he is terrified. He hovers over the sandy monument to protect it. He blocks the waves from the walls he has made. Salt-water soaked and shivering he snarls at the incoming tide.

"It's my castle," he defies.

The ocean need not respond. Both know to whom the sand belongs.

Finally the cliff of water mounts high above the man and his little empire. For just a moment he is shadowed by the wall of water . . . then it crashes. His tiny towers of triumph crumble and disperse and he is left on his knees . . . clutching muddy handfuls of yesterday.

If only he had known. If only he had listened. If only . . .

But he, like most, never listens.

Jesus describes these people, the unprepared, by saying they know nothing about what will happen. They aren't cruel. They aren't rebellious or angry at God.

But they are blind. They don't see the setting sun. And they are deaf. They don't hear the pounding waves.

During the last week of his life, Jesus took valuable time to tell us to learn the lesson of the waves and prepare for the end.

Remember, the reason we are studying the last week of Christ is to see what is on his heart. Hear what he says. See who he touches. Witness what he does. We've seen his compassion for the forgotten. We've seen his contempt for the fake. Now a third passion surfaces; his concern for our readiness. "No one knows when that day or time will be, not the angels in heaven, not even the Son. Only the Father knows."[1]

His message is unmistakable: He will return, but no one knows when. So, be ready.

It's the message of the parable of the virgins.[2]

It's the message of the parable of the talents.[3]

It's the message of the parable of the sheep and the goats.[4]

It's a message we must heed.

But it is a message often ignored.

I was reminded of this not long ago when I boarded a plane. I walked down the aisle, found my seat, and sat down next to a strange sight.

The man seated next to me was in a robe and slippers. He was dressed for the living room, not for a journey. His seat was odd, too. Whereas my seat was the cloth type you normally see, his was fine leather.

"Imported," he said, when he noticed I was looking. "Bought it in Argentina and put it on myself."

Before I could speak he pointed to some inlaid stones in the armrest. "The rubies I purchased in Africa. They cost me a fortune."

That was only the beginning. His fold-down table was of mahogany. There was a portable TV installed next to the window. A tiny ceiling fan and globed light hung above us.

I had never seen anything like it.

My question was the obvious one, "Why did you spend so much time and expense on an airline seat?"

"I live here," he explained. "I make my home on the plane."

"You never get off?"

"Never! How could I deboard and leave such comfort?"

Incredible. The man made a home out of a mode of transportation. He made a residence out of a journey. Hard to believe? You think I'm stretching the truth? Well, maybe I haven't seen such foolishness in a plane, but I have in life. And so have you.

You've seen people treat this world like it was a permanent home. It's not. You've seen people pour time and energy into life like it will last forever. It won't. You've seen people so proud of what they have done, that they hope they will never have to leave— they will.

We all will. We are in transit. Someday the plane will stop and the de-boarding will begin.

Wise are those who are ready when the pilot says to get off.

I don't know much, but I do know how to travel. Carry little. Eat light. Take a nap. And get off when you reach the city.

And I don't know much about sandcastles. But children do. Watch them and learn. Go ahead and build, but build with a child's heart. When the sun sets and the tides take—applaud. Salute the process of life, take your father's hand, and go home.

Chapter 18

Be Ready

"So always be ready,
because you don't know the day your Lord will come."
Matthew 24:42

There is a secret to wearing a vest.

It's a secret every father should tell his son. It's one of those manly things that has to be passed down from generation to generation. It rates up there with teaching your son to shave and use deodorant. It's a secret every vest wearer must know. If you own a vest, I hope you know it. If you own and vest and don't know it, here it is: Button the first button correctly.

Take your time. Don't be in a rush. Look carefully in the mirror and then match the right button with the right hole.

If you do, if you get the first button buttoned right, then the rest will follow suit (excuse the pun). If, however, you don't get the first button right, every button thereafter will be buttoned incorrectly. The result will be a lopsided vest. Put the second button in the top hole or slide the second hole over the top button and, well, it just won't work.

There are certain things in life done only one way. Buttoning a vest is one of them.

Being ready is another.

According to Jesus, being ready for his return is a vest-button principle. According to Jesus, start wrong on this first move and the rest of your life will be cockeyed.

Not everything is a vest-button truth. The church you attend isn't. The Bible translation you read isn't. The ministry you select isn't. But being ready for Jesus' return is a vest-button truth. Get this right and the rest will fall into place. Miss it and get ready for some wrinkles.

How do we know this is a vest-button principle? Jesus told us. According to Matthew, Jesus told us in the last sermon he ever preached.

It may surprise you that Jesus made preparedness the theme of his last sermon. It did me. I would have preached on love or family or the importance of church. Jesus didn't. Jesus preached on what many today consider to be old-fashioned. He preached on being ready for heaven and staying out of hell.

It's his message when he tells of the wise and the foolish servant.[1] The wise one was ready for the return of the master, the foolish one was not.

It's his message when he tells about the ten bridesmaids. Five were wise and five were foolish.[2] The wise ones were ready when the groom came and the foolish ones were at the corner store looking for more oil.

It's his message when he tells of the three servants and the bags of gold.[3] Two servants put the money to work and made more money for the master. The third hid his in a hole. The first two were ready and rewarded when the master returned. The third was unprepared and punished.

Be ready. It's a first step, non-negotiable, vest-button principle.

That is the theme of Jesus' last sermon, "So always be ready, because you don't know the day your Lord will come."[4] He didn't tell when the day of the Lord would be, but he did describe what the day would be like. It's a day no one will miss.

Every person who has ever lived will be present at that final gathering. Every heart that has ever beat. Every mouth that has ever spoken. On that day you will be surrounded by a sea of people. Rich, poor. Famous, unknown. Kings, bums. Brilliant, demented. All will be present. And all will be looking in one direction. All will be looking at him. Every human being.

"The Son of Man will come again in his great glory."[5]

You won't look at anyone else. No side glances to see what others are wearing. No whispers about new jewelry or comments about who is present. At this, the greatest gathering in history, you will have eyes for only one—the Son of Man. Wrapped in splendor. Shot through with radiance. Imploded with light and magnetic in power.

Jesus describes this day with certainty.

He leaves no room for doubt. He doesn't say he may return, or might return, but that he *will* return. By the way, one-twentieth of your New Testament speaks about his return. There are over three hundred references to his second coming. Twenty-three of the twenty-seven New Testament books speak of it. And they speak of it with confidence.

"You also must be ready, because the Son of Man will come at a time you don't expect him."[6]

". . . Jesus, who has been taken from you into heaven, will come back in the same way you have seen him go into heaven."[7]

". . . he will come a second time, not to offer himself for sin, but to bring salvation to those who are waiting for him."[8]

". . . the day of the Lord will come like a thief in the night."[9]

His return is certain.

His return is final.

Upon his return "he will separate them into two groups as a shepherd separates the sheep from the goats. The Son of Man will put the sheep on his right and the goats on his left."[10]

The word *separate* is a sad word. To separate a mother from a daughter, a father from a son, a husband from a wife. To separate people on earth is sorrowful, but to think of it being done for eternity is horrible.

Especially when one group is destined for heaven and the other group is going to hell.

We don't like to talk about hell, do we? In intellectual circles the topic of hell is regarded as primitive and foolish. It's not logical. "A loving God wouldn't send people to hell." So we dismiss it.

But to dismiss it is to dismiss a core teaching of Jesus. The doctrine of hell is not one developed by Paul, Peter, or John. It is taught by Jesus himself.

And to dismiss it is to dismiss much more. It is to dismiss the presence of a loving God and the privilege of a free choice. Let me explain.

We are free either to love God or not. He invites us to love him. He urges us to love him. He came that we might love him. But, in the end, the choice is yours and mine. To take that choice from each of us, for him to force us to love him, would be less than love.

God explains the benefits, outlines the promises, and articulates very clearly the consequences. And then, in the end, he leaves the choice to us.

Hell was not prepared for people. Hell "was prepared for the devil and his angels."[11] For a person to go to hell, then, is for a person to go against God's intended destiny. "God has not destined us to the terrors of judgment, but to the full attainment of salvation through our Lord Jesus Christ." [12] Hell is man's choice, not God's choice.

Consider, then, this explanation of hell: Hell is the chosen place of the person who loves self more than God, who loves sin more than his Savior, who loves this world more than God's world. Judgment is that moment when God looks at the rebellious and says, "Your choice will be honored."

To reject the dualistic outcome of history and say there is no hell leaves gaping holes in any banner of a just God. To say there is no hell is to say God condones the rebellious, unrepentant heart. To say there is no hell is to portray God with eyes blind to the hunger and evil in the world. To say there is no hell is to say that God doesn't care that people are beaten and massacred, that he doesn't care that women are raped or families wrecked. To say there is no hell is to say God has no justice, no sense of right and wrong, and eventually to say God has no love. For true love hates what is evil.

Hell is the ultimate expression of a just Creator.

The parables of the wise and loyal servant, the wise and foolish bridesmaids, and loyal and wicked servants, all point to the same conclusion: "Everyone must die once and be judged."[13] *Eternity is to be taken seriously.* A judgment is coming.

Our task on earth is singular—to choose our eternal home. You can afford many wrong choices in life. You can choose the wrong career and survive, the wrong city and survive, the wrong house and survive. You can even choose the wrong mate and survive. But there is one choice that must be made correctly and that is your eternal destiny.

It's interesting that Jesus' first and last sermon have the same message. In his first sermon, the Sermon on the Mount, Jesus calls you and me to choose between the rock and the sand,[14] the wide gate and the narrow gate, the wide road and the narrow road, the big crowd and the small crowd, the certainty of hell and the joy of heaven.[15] In his last sermon he calls us to do the same. He calls us to be ready.

While on one of his expeditions to the Antarctic, Sir Ernest Shackleton left some of his men on Elephant Island with the intent of returning for them and carrying them back to England. But he was delayed. By the time he could go back for them the sea had frozen and he had no access to the island. Three times he tried to reach them, but was prevented by the ice. Finally, on his fourth try, he broke through and found a narrow channel.

Much to his surprise, he found the crewmen waiting for him, supplies packed and ready to board. They were soon on their way back to England. He asked them how they knew to be ready for him. They told him they didn't know when he would return, but they were sure he would. So every morning, the leader rolled up his bag and packed his gear and told the crew to do the same saying, "Get your things ready, boys, the boss may come today."[16]

The crew leader did his crew a favor by keeping them prepared.

Jesus has done us a service by urging us to do the same: Be ready. It's a vest-button principle. Get that one buttoned right today. For you don't want to be fumbling with buttons in the presence of God.

Chapter 19

The People
with the
Roses

John Blanchard stood up from the bench, straightened his Army uniform, and studied the crowd of people making their way through Grand Central Station. He looked for the girl whose heart he knew, but whose face he didn't, the girl with the rose.

His interest in her had begun thirteen months before in a Florida library. Taking a book off the shelf he found himself intrigued, not with the words of the book, but with the notes penciled in the margin. The soft handwriting reflected a thoughtful soul and insightful mind. In the front of the book, he discovered the previous owner's name, Miss Hollis Maynell.

With time and effort he located her address. She lived in New York City. He wrote her a letter introducing himself and inviting her to correspond. The next day he was shipped overseas for service in World War II. During the next year and one month the two grew to know each other through the mail. Each letter was a seed falling on a fertile heart. A romance was budding.

Blanchard requested a photograph, but she refused. She felt that if he really cared, it wouldn't matter what she looked like.

When the day finally came for him to return from Europe, they scheduled their first meeting—7:00 P.M. at the Grand Central Station in New York. "You'll recognize me," she wrote, "by the red rose I'll be wearing on my lapel."

So at 7:00 he was in the station looking for a girl whose heart he loved, but whose face he'd never seen.

I'll let Mr. Blanchard tell you what happened.

A young woman was coming toward me, her figure long and slim. Her blonde hair lay back in curls from her delicate ears; her eyes were blue as flowers. Her lips and chin had a gentle firmness, and in her pale green suit she was like springtime come alive. I started toward her, entirely forgetting to notice that she was not wearing a rose. As I moved, a small, provocative smile curved her lips. "Going my way, sailor?" she murmured.

Almost uncontrollably I made one step closer to her, and then I saw Hollis Maynell.

She was standing almost directly behind the girl. A woman well past 40, she had graying hair tucked under a worn hat. She was more than plump, her thick-ankled feet thrust into low-heeled shoes. The girl in the green suit was walking quickly away. I felt as though I was split in two, so keen was my desire to follow her, and yet so deep was my longing for the woman whose spirit had truly companioned me and upheld my own.

And there she stood. Her pale, plump face was gentle and sensible, her gray eyes had a warm and kindly twinkle. I did not hesitate. My finger gripped the small worn blue leather copy of the book that was to identify me to her. This would not be love, but it would be something precious, something perhaps even better than love, a friendship for which I had been and must ever be grateful.

I squared my shoulders and saluted and held out the book to the woman, even though while I spoke I felt choked by the bitterness of my disappointment. "I'm Lieutenant John Blanchard, and you must be Miss Maynell. I am so glad you could meet me; may I take you to dinner?"

The woman's face broadened into a tolerant smile. "I don't know what this is about, son," she answered, "but the young lady in the green suit who just went by, she begged me to wear this rose on my coat. And she said if you were to ask me out to dinner, I should go and tell you that she is waiting for you in the big restaurant across the street. She said it was some kind of test!" [1]

It's not difficult to understand and admire Miss Maynell's wisdom. The true nature of a heart is seen in its response to the unattractive. "Tell me whom you love," Houssaye wrote, "and I will tell you who you are."

Hollis Maynell, however, is far from the first person to gauge a heart by a person's concern for the undesirable.

In the last sermon recorded by Matthew, Jesus does exactly that. He does it not with a parable, but with a description. He doesn't tell a story, but he describes a scene—the last scene, the final judgment. In his final discourse, he puts into words the very message he has put into actions, "Love for the least."

We saw in the last chapter the significance of the final judgment. We saw its certainty—there is no doubt as to Jesus' return. We saw its totality—everyone will be there. And we saw its finality—for on that day Jesus will separate the sheep from the goats, the good from the wicked.

On what basis will he make his selection? The answer may surprise you. "I was hungry, and you gave me food. I was thirsty, and you gave me something to drink. I was alone and away from home, and you invited me into your house. I was without clothes, and you gave me something to wear. I was sick, and you cared for me. I was in prison, and you visited me."[2]

What is the sign of the saved? Their scholarship? Their willingness to go to foreign lands? Their ability to amass an audience and preach? Their skillful pens and hope-filled volumes? Their great miracles? No.

The sign of the saved is their love for the least.

Those put on the right hand of God will be those who gave food to the hungry, drink to the thirsty, warmth to the lonely, clothing to the naked, comfort to the sick, and friendship to the imprisoned.

The sign of the saved is their love for the least.

Did you note how simple the works are? Jesus doesn't say, "I was sick and you healed me. . . . I was in prison and you liberated me. . . . I was lonely and you built a retirement home for me. . . ." He doesn't say, "I was thirsty and you gave me spiritual counsel."

No fanfare. No hoopla. No media coverage. Just good people doing good things.

For when we do good things to others we do good things to God.

When Francis of Asissi turned his back on wealth to seek God in simplicity, he stripped naked and walked out of the city. He soon encountered a leper on the side of the road. He passed him, then stopped and went back and embraced the diseased man. Francis then continued on his journey. After a few steps he turned to look again at the leper, but no one was there.

For the rest of his life, he believed the leper was Jesus Christ. He may have been right.

Jesus lives in the forgotten. He has taken up residence in the ignored. He has made a mansion amidst the ill. If we want to see God we must go among the broken and beaten and there we will see him.

"He rewards those who truly want to find him,"[3] is the promise. "Anything you did for even the least of my people here, you also did for me,"[4] is the plan.

Perhaps you read about the fellow in Philadelphia who went to the flea market and found a frame he liked. It was only a couple of bucks, this dusty print of a country church. It was torn and faded, but the guy liked the frame so he bought it.

When he got home he opened it up and out tumbled a neatly folded sheet of paper. It was the Declaration of Independence. What everyone had thought was a two-dollar painting at a flea market actually contained one of the original one hundred copies of the Declaration of Independence printed on July 4, 1776.[5]

Valuable surprises are discovered in unlikely sources. True in flea markets and true in life. Make an investment in the people the world has cast off—the homeless, the AIDS patient, the orphan, the divorcee—and you may discover the source of your independence.

Jesus' message is stirring: "The way you treat them is the way you treat me."

Of all the teachings during the last week of Christ, this one is for me the most penetrating. I wish he hadn't said what he said. I wish he'd said that the sign of the saved is the books they have written, for I've written several. I wish he'd said the sign of the saved was the numbers of sermons they've preached, for I've preached hundreds. I wish he'd said the sign of the saved was the audiences they've amassed, for I've spoken to thousands.

But he didn't. His words reminded me that the person who sees Christ is the one who sees the hurting person. To see Jesus, go to the convalescent home, sit down beside the elderly woman, and steady her hand as she puts the spoon in her mouth. To see Jesus, go to the community hospital and ask the nurse to take you to see one who has received no visits. To see Jesus, leave your office and go down the hall and talk to the man who is regretting his divorce and missing his children. To see Jesus, go to the inner city and give a sandwich—not a sermon, but a sandwich—to the bag lady who's made a home out of an overpass.

To see Jesus . . . see the unattractive and forgotten.

You might say it is a test. A test to measure the depth of our character. The same kind of test Hollis Maynell used with John Blanchard. The rejected of the world wear the roses. Sometimes we, like John Blanchard, have to adjust our expectations. Sometimes we have to re-examine our motives.

Had he turned his back on the unattractive, he would have missed the love of his life.

If we turn our backs, we will miss even more.

Chapter 20

Served by the Best

"The master will dress himself to serve and tell the servants to sit at the table, and he will serve them."
Luke 12:37

*L*et's suppose something really crazy happened. Let's suppose you were invited to a dinner with the president.

There you are stacking dishes in the kitchen of the restaurant where you work the evening shift when a courier arrives at the back door.

"The owner won't be back until tomorrow," you tell him.

"I'm not looking for the owner, I'm looking for you."

"Huh?"

"I'm from the White House," he says, which explains the dark suit and briefcase.

"Are you for real?" You look twice at him and once behind him as he opens his case.

"I came to deliver this letter."

Part of you wonders what you've done wrong. Another part of you wonders if this isn't a joke your cousin Alfred is playing to get back at you for the horseradish in his car. And all of you thinks this guy has the wrong guy.

But you dry your hands on your apron and take the letter. It's a personal letter. There is an emblem on the envelope and your name is written, not typed, in cursive.

The stationery is the heavy expensive type which blows the Cousin Alfred theory; he's too cheap to buy this. It couldn't be a bill, collectors aren't this formal. You open the letter and, well, how-do-you-do, it's a letter from the president of the United States of America.

You look up at the fellow who brought it and he's smiling like this is the part of his job he likes the best.

You look around in the kitchen for somebody to show it to but you're alone. You think about running into the restaurant and sharing it with Alma the waitress, but you can't because you are too curious to wait. So you read the letter.

It's an invitation—an invitation to a dinner. A state dinner. A dinner given in your honor. A dinner dedicated to you.

Your ex threw you a surprise party during the first year of your marriage, but besides that you can't remember when someone has had a dinner for you. Not the kids. Not the neighbors. Not your boss . . . you don't even know if you've ever given yourself a dinner in your honor.

And now the commander in chief wants to.

"What's the catch?" you ask.

"No catch, just a request that you come to the White House. May I give the president your response?"

"Huh?"

"May I give the president your answer? Can you come to the dinner?"

"Well, of cuh-cuh-course. I'd love to go."

And so you go. On the appointed night, you put on your best and you go to Pennsylvania Avenue. You are met out front by more black suits who escort you in. Inside the doors a garcon of sorts takes over. Your steps echo as you follow the tuxedoed guide down the tall hall lined with portraits of past presidents.

At the end of the corridor is the banquet room. In the center of the room is a long table and in the center of the table is one plate and beside the plate is one name—yours.

The attendant motions for you to sit and when you do he leaves and you do the thing you've wanted to do since you stepped in to the residence. You look around you and say, "Wow."

You've never seen a table this long. You've never seen crystal this nice. You never seen china this valuable. You've never seen a setting with so many forks or a candelabra with so many candles.

"Wow."

Under your feet is an Oriental rug. Probably came from China. Over your head is a chandelier with a billion pieces of glass. *I bet it's German.* The table and chairs are made of polished teak. *Indian, no doubt.*

Straight ahead is a hearth with a fire and a white mantle. Above the mantle is a painting—a painting of, gulp, a painting of you! That's you up there. Same eyes, same goofy smile, same nose you wish was half the size—that's you!

"Wow."

"I keep it in here so I can remember you."

The voice from behind startles you. You don't have to turn and look to see who it is—there is only one voice like his. You wait until he is right beside you before you look up. You know he's there because he places his hand on your shoulder.

You turn and look and there he is, the president. A bit shorter than you imagined, but every bit as authoritative. The square jaw. The deep eyes. The high cheeks. The gray suit. The red tie. The apron.

The what?

The president is wearing an apron! A common kitchen apron just like the one you wear when you work.

And, as if that isn't enough, behind him is a dinner cart. He reaches for your bread plate and gives you a dinner roll. "I'm so glad you could come and be my guest."

You know you should say something but what you were going to say is forgotten somewhere between the last "Wow" you said and the first *What's going on here* you thought.

You thought it was shocking to get the invitation. You thought it was breathtaking to see the White House. Your jaw hit the floor when you saw your picture on the wall. But all of that was nothing compared this.

The commander in chief as a waiter? The president serving you food? The chief executive bringing wine and bread to your table? All those neatly prepared compliments and carefully rehearsed accolades are forgotten and you blurt out what is really on your mind: "Wait a minute. This isn't right. You aren't supposed to be doing this—I am. You aren't supposed to be serving me. I'm the dishwasher. I work at the diner. You're the top dog. Let me have the apron and let me put the food on the table, . . . Sir."

But he won't let you. "Keep your seat," he insists. "Today I honor you."

I warned you this was a crazy story. This kind of stuff doesn't happen . . . or does it?

It does for those who see it. For those aware of it, it happens every week. In banquet halls around the world the commander honors the common. There they are—regular folk right out of the kitchens and car pools of life, seated at the chief's table.

The honored guests. VIPs. Hosted and served by the one in charge of history.

"This is my body," he says as he breaks the bread.

And you thought it was a ritual. You thought it was just an observance. You thought it was a memorial to something which was done back then. You thought it was a re-enactment of a meal he had with them.

It is so much more.

It is a meal he has with you.

When I was a young boy I was a part of a church corps which took communion to the shut-ins and hospitalized. We visited those who were unable to come to church but still desired to pray and partake of communion.

I must have been ten or eleven years of age when we went to one hospital room that housed an elderly gentleman who was very weak. He was asleep, so we tried to wake him. We couldn't. We shook him, we spoke to him, we tapped him on the shoulder, but we couldn't stir him.

We hated to leave without performing our duty, but we didn't know what to do.

One of the young guys with me observed that even though the man was asleep his mouth was open. Why not? we said. So we prayed over the cracker and stuck a piece on his tongue. Then we prayed over the grape juice and poured it down his mouth.

He never woke up.

Neither do many today. For some, communion is a sleepy hour in which wafers are eaten and juice is drinken and the soul never stirs. It wasn't intended to be as such.

It was intended to be an I-can't-believe-it's-me-pinch-me-I'm-dreaming invitation to sit at God's table and be served by the King himself.

When you read Matthew's account of the Last Supper, one incredible truth surfaces. Jesus is the person behind it all. It was Jesus who selected the place, designated the time, and set the meal in order. "The chosen time is near. I will have the Passover with my followers at your house."[1]

And at the Supper, Jesus is not a guest, but the host. "And [Jesus] gave to the disciples." The subject of the verbs is the message of the event: "he took . . . he blessed . . . he broke . . . he gave. . . ."

And, at the Supper, Jesus is not the served, but the servant. It is Jesus who, during the Supper, put on the garb of a servant and washed the disciples' feet.[2]

Jesus is the most active one at the table. Jesus is not portrayed as the one who reclines and receives, but as the one who stands and gives.

He still does. The Lord's Supper is a gift to you. The Lord's Supper is a sacrament[3] not a sacrifice.[4]

Often, we think of the Supper as a performance, a time when we are on stage and God is the audience. A ceremony in which we do the work and he does the watching. That's not how it was intended. If it was, Jesus would have taken his seat at the table and relaxed.[5]

That's not what he did. He, instead, fulfilled his role as a rabbi by guiding his disciples through the Passover. He fulfilled his role as a servant by washing their feet. And he fulfilled his role as a Savior by granting them forgiveness of sins.

He was in charge. He was on center stage. He was the person behind and in the moment.

And he still is.

It is the Lord's table you sit at. It is the Lord's Supper you eat. Just as Jesus prayed for his disciples, Jesus begs God for us.[6] When you are called to the table, it might be an emissary who gives the letter, but it is Jesus who wrote it.

It is a holy invitation. A sacred sacrament bidding you to leave the chores of life and enter his splendor.

He meets you at the table.

And when the bread is broken, Christ breaks it. When the wine is poured, Christ pours it. And when your burdens are lifted, it is because the King in the apron has drawn near.

Think about that the next time you go to the table.

One last thought.

What happens on earth is just a warm-up for what will happen in heaven.[7] So the next time the messenger calls you to the table, drop what you are doing and go. Be blessed and be fed and, most importantly, be sure you're still eating at his table when he calls us home.

Chapter 21

He Chose You

"*Sit here while I go over there and pray. . . .*
My soul is overwhelmed with sorrow to the point of death.
Matthew 26:36,38, NIV

"*I pray for these followers, but I am also praying*
for all those who will believe in me because of their teaching."
John 17:20

*T*hursday night. Midnight.

The week has been full of finalities. The final visit to the temple. The final sermon. The final supper. And now, the most emotional hour of the week, the final prayer.

The garden is in shadows. The olive trees are knotted and gnarled. They twist five or six feet into the sky. Roots sprawl from the trunks and claw deeply into the rocky soil.

The spring moon casts the garden in silver. Constellations sparkle against the black velvet of the night sky. Fleets of clouds float. A breeze cools. Insects sing. Leaves stir.

That's him. Jesus. In the grove. On the ground. The young man. The one in the sweat-soaked garment. Kneeling. Imploring. His hair is plastered to his wet forehead. He agonizes.

A sound is heard in the trees. Snoring. Jesus looks across the garden at the dearest friends he has—they are asleep. They lean against the broad trunks and slumber. His yearnings don't stir them. His distress doesn't move them. They are tired.

He stands and walks through the shadowed trees and squats before them. "Please," he asks, "please just stay awake with me."

The Lord of the universe doesn't want to be alone.

He can understand their weariness, though. He has given them more in the last few hours than they could possibly grasp. Never had the apostles known Jesus to talk so much. Never had they seen him speak with such urgency. His words were fervent, fiery.

Thursday night . . . a few hours earlier.

It's nearly midnight when they leave the upper room and descend through the streets of the city. They pass the Lower Pool and exit the Fountain Gate and walk out of Jerusalem. The roads are lined with the fires and tents of Passover pilgrims. Most are asleep, heavied with the evening meal. Those still awake think little of the band of men walking the chalky road.

They pass through the valley and ascend the path which will take them to Gethsemane. The road is steep so they stop to rest. Somewhere within the city walls the twelfth apostle darts down a street. His feet have been washed by the man he will betray. His heart has been claimed by the Evil One he has heard. He runs to find Caiaphas.

The final encounter of the battle has begun.

As Jesus looks at the city of Jerusalem, he sees what the disciples can't. It is here, on the outskirts of Jerusalem, that the battle will end. He sees the staging of Satan. He sees the dashing of the demons. He sees the Evil One preparing for the final encounter. The enemy lurks as a spectre over the hour. Satan, the host of hatred, has seized the heart of Judas and whispered in the ear of Caiaphas. Satan, the master of death, has opened the caverns and prepared to receive the source of light.

Hell is breaking loose.

History records it as a battle of the Jews against Jesus. It wasn't. It was a battle of God against Satan.

And Jesus knew it. He knew that before the war was over, he would be taken captive. He knew that before victory would come defeat. He knew that before the throne would come the cup. He knew that before the light of Sunday would come the blackness of Friday.

And he is afraid.

He turns and begins the final ascent to the garden. When he reaches the entry he stops and turns his eyes toward his circle of friends. It will be the last time he sees them before they abandon him. He knows what they will do when the soldiers come. He knows their betrayal is only minutes away.

But he doesn't accuse. He doesn't lecture. Instead, he prays. His last moments with his disciples are in prayer. And the words he speaks are as eternal as the stars which hear them.

Imagine, for a moment, yourself in this situation. Your final hour with a son about to be sent overseas. Your last moments with your dying spouse. One last visit with your parent. What do you say? What do you do? What words do you choose?

It's worth noting that Jesus chose prayer. He chose to pray for us. "I pray for these men. But I am also praying for all people who will believe in me because of the teaching of these men. Father, I pray that all people who believe in me can be one. . . . I pray that these people can also be one in us, so that the world will believe that you sent me."[1]

You need to note that in this final prayer, Jesus prayed for you. You need to underline in red and highlight in yellow his love: "I am also praying for all people who will believe in me because of the teaching." That is you. As Jesus stepped into the garden, you were in his prayers. As Jesus looked into heaven, you were in his vision. As Jesus dreamed of the day when we will be where he is, he saw you there.

His final prayer was about you. His final pain was for you. His final passion was you.

He then turns, steps into the garden, and invites Peter, James, and John to come. He tells them his soul is "overwhelmed with sorrow to the point of death," and begins to pray.

Never has he felt so alone. What must be done, only he can do. An angel can't do it. No angel has the power to break open hell's gates. A man can't do it. No man has the purity to destroy sin's claim. No force on earth can face the force of evil and win—except God.

"The spirit is willing, but the flesh is weak," Jesus confesses.

His humanity begged to be delivered from what his divinity could see. Jesus, the carpenter, implores. Jesus, the man, peers into the dark pit and begs, "Can't there be another way?"

Did he know the answer before he asked the question? Did his human heart hope his heavenly father had found another way? We don't know. But we do know he asked to get out. We do know he begged for an exit. We do know there was a time when if he could have, he would have turned his back on the whole mess and gone away.

But he couldn't.

He couldn't because he saw you. Right there in the middle of a world which isn't fair. He saw you cast into a river of life you didn't request. He saw you betrayed by those you love. He saw you with a body which gets sick and a heart which grows weak.

He saw you in your own garden of gnarled trees and sleeping friends. He saw you staring into the pit of your own failures and the mouth of your own grave.

He saw you in your Garden of Gethsemane—and he didn't want you to be alone.

He wanted you to know that he has been there, too. He knows

what it's like to be plotted against. He knows what it's like to be confused. He knows what it's like to be torn between two desires. He knows what it's like to smell the stench of Satan. And, perhaps most of all, he knows what it's like to beg God to change his mind and to hear God say so gently, but firmly, "No."

For that is what God says to Jesus. And Jesus accepts the answer. At some moment during that midnight hour an angel of mercy comes over the weary body of the man in the garden. As he stands, the anguish is gone from his eyes. His fist will clench no more. His heart will fight no more.

The battle is won. You may have thought it was won on Golgotha. It wasn't. You may have thought the sign of victory is the empty tomb. It isn't. The final battle was won in Gethsemane. And the sign of conquest is Jesus at peace in the olive trees.

For it was in the garden that he made his decision. He would rather go to hell for you than go to heaven without you.

Chapter 22

When Your World Turns against You

*"In the future you will see the Son of Man
sitting at the right hand of God."*
Matthew 26:64

Get up, we must go. Here comes the man who has turned against me."[1]

The words were spoken to Judas. But they could have been spoken to anyone. They could have been spoken to John, to Peter, to James. They could have been spoken to Thomas, to Andrew, to Nathaniel. They could have been spoken to the Roman soldiers, to the Jewish leaders. They could have been spoken to Pilate, to Herod, to Caiaphas. They could have been spoken to every person who praised him last Sunday but abandoned him tonight.

Everyone turned against Jesus that night. Everyone.

Judas did. What was your motive Judas? Why did you do it? Were you trying to call his hand? Did you want the money? Were you seeking some attention? And why, dear Judas, why did it have to be a kiss? You could have pointed. You could have just called his name. But you put your lips to his cheek and kissed. A snake kills with his mouth.

The people did. The crowd turned on Jesus. We wonder who was in the crowd. Who were the bystanders? Matthew just says they were people. Regular folks like you and me with bills to pay and kids to raise and jobs to do. Individually they never would have turned on Jesus, but collectively they wanted to kill him. Even the instantaneous healing of an amputated ear didn't sway them. They suffered from mob blindness. They blocked each other's vision of Jesus.

The disciples did. "All of Jesus' followers left him and ran away."[2] Matthew must have written those words slowly. He was in that group. All the disciples were. Jesus told them they would scamper. They vowed they wouldn't. But they did. When the choice came between their skin and their friend they chose to run. Oh, they stood for a while. Peter even pulled his sword, went for the neck, and got a lobe. But their courage was as fleeting as their feet. When they saw Jesus was going down, they got out.

The religious leaders did. Not surprising. Disappointing, though. They are the spiritual leaders of the nation. Men entrusted with the dispensing of goodness. Role models for the children. The pastors and Bible teachers of the community. "The leading priests and the whole Jewish council tried to find something false against Jesus so they could kill him."[3] Paint that passage black with injustice. Paint the arrest green with jealousy. Paint that scene red with innocent blood.

And paint Peter in a corner. For that's where he is. No place to go. Caught in his own mistake. Peter did exactly what he had said he wouldn't do. He had promised fervently only hours before, "Everyone else may stumble in their faith because of you, but I will not!" I hope Peter was hungry, because he ate those words.

Everyone turned against Jesus.

Though the kiss was planted by Judas, the betrayal was committed by all. Every person took a step, but no one took a stand. As Jesus left the garden he walked alone. The world had turned against him. He was betrayed.

Betray. The word is an eighth of an inch above *betroth* in the dictionary, but a world from "betroth" in life. It's a weapon found only in the hands of one you love. Your enemy has no such tool, for only a friend can betray. Betrayal is mutiny. It's a violation of a trust, an inside job.

Would that it were a stranger. Would that it were a random attack. Would that you were a victim of circumstances. But you aren't. You are a victim of a friend.

A sandpaper kiss is placed on your cheek. A promise is made with fingers crossed. You look to your friends and your friends don't look back. You look to the system for justice—the system looks to you as a scapegoat.

You are betrayed. Bitten with a snake's kiss.

It's more than rejection. Rejection opens a wound, betrayal pours the salt.

It's more than loneliness. Loneliness leaves you in the cold, betrayal closes the door.

It's more than mockery. Mockery plunges the knife, betrayal twists it.

It's more than an insult. An insult attacks your pride, betrayal breaks your heart.

As I search for betrayal's synonyms, I keep seeing betrayal's victims. That unsigned letter in yesterday's mail, "My husband just told me he had an affair two years ago," she wrote. "I feel so alone." The phone call at home from the elderly woman whose drug-addicted son had taken her money. My friend in the Midwest who moved his family to take the promised job that never materialized. The single mother whose ex-husband brings his new girlfriend to her house when he comes to get the kids for the weekend. The seven-year-old girl infected with the HIV virus. "I'm mad at my mother," were her words.

Betrayal . . . when your world turns against you.

Betrayal . . . where there is opportunity for love, there is opportunity for hurt.

When betrayal comes, what do you do? Get out? Get angry? Get even? You have to deal with it some way. Let's see how Jesus dealt with it.

Begin by noticing how Jesus saw Judas. "Jesus answered, 'Friend, do what you came to do.' "[4]

Of all the names I would have chosen for Judas it would not have been "friend." What Judas did to Jesus was grossly unfair. There is no indication that Jesus ever mistreated Judas. There is no clue that Judas was ever left out or neglected. When, during the Last Supper, Jesus told the disciples that his betrayer sat at the table, they didn't turn to one another and whisper, "It's Judas. Jesus told us he would do this."

They didn't whisper it because Jesus never said it. He had known it. He had known what Judas would do, but he treated the betrayer as if he was faithful.

It's even more unfair when you consider the betrayal was Judas's idea. The religious leaders didn't seek him, Judas sought them. "What will you pay me for giving Jesus to you?" he asked.[5] The betrayal would have been more palatable had Judas been propositioned by the leaders, but he wasn't. He propositioned them.

And Judas's method . . . again, why did it have to be a kiss?[6]

And why did he have to call him "Teacher"?[7] That's a title of respect. The incongruity of his words, deeds, and actions—I wouldn't have called Judas "friend."

But that is exactly what Jesus called him. Why? Jesus could see something we can't. Let me explain.

There was once a person in our world who brought Denalyn and me a lot of stress. She would call in the middle of the night. She was demanding and ruthless. She screamed at us in public. When she wanted something she wanted it immediately and she wanted it exclusively from us.

But we never asked her to leave us alone. We never told her to bug someone else. We never tried to get even.

After all, she was only a few months old.

It was easy for us to forgive our infant daughter's behavior because we knew she didn't know better.

Now, there is a world of difference between an innocent child and a deliberate Judas. But there is still a point to my story and it is this: The way to handle a person's behavior is to understand the cause of it. One way to deal with a person's peculiarities is to try to understand why they are peculiar.

Jesus knew Judas had been seduced by a powerful foe. He was aware of the wiles of Satan's whispers (he had just heard them himself). He knew how hard it was for Judas to do what was right.

He didn't justify what Judas did. He didn't minimize the deed. Nor did he release Judas from his choice. But he did look eye to eye with his betrayer and try to understand.

As long as you hate your enemy, a jail door is closed and a prisoner is taken. But when you try to understand and release your foe from your hatred, then the prisoner is released and that prisoner is you.

Perhaps you don't like that idea. Perhaps the thought of forgiveness is unrealistic. Perhaps the idea of trying to understand the Judases in our world is simply too gracious.

My response to you then is a question. What do you suggest? Will harboring the anger solve the problem? Will getting even remove the hurt? Does hatred do any good? Again, I'm not minimizing your hurt or justifying their actions. But I am saying that justice won't come this side of eternity. And demanding that your enemy get his or her share of pain will, in the process, be most painful to you.

May I gently but firmly remind you of something you know but may have forgotten? Life is not fair.

That's not pessimism, it's fact. That's not a complaint, it's just the way things are. I don't like it. Neither do you. We want life to be fair. Ever since the kid down the block got a bike and we didn't, we've been saying the same thing, "That's not fair."

But at some point someone needs to say to us, "Who ever told you life was going to be fair?"

God didn't. He didn't say, "*If* you have many kinds of troubles," he said, "*When* you have many kinds of troubles."[8] Troubles are part of the package. Betrayals are part of our troubles. Don't be surprised when betrayals come. Don't look for fairness here—look instead where Jesus looked.

Jesus looked to the future. Read his words: "In the future you will see the Son of Man coming." While going through hell, Jesus kept his eyes on heaven. While surrounded by enemies he kept his mind on his father. While abandoned on earth, he kept his heart on home. "In the future you will see the Son of Man sitting at the right hand of God, the Powerful One, and coming on clouds in the sky."[9]

I took a snow skiing lesson some time back. My instructor said I had potential but poor perspective. He said I looked at my skis too much. I told him I had to. They kept going where I didn't want them to go. "Does it help?" he asked.

"I guess not," I confessed, "I still fall a lot."

He gestured toward the splendid mountains on the horizon. "Try looking out there as you ski. Keep your eyes on the mountains and you'll keep your balance." He was right. It worked.

The best way to keep your balance is to to keep your focus on another horizon. That's what Jesus did.

"My kingdom does not belong to this world," Jesus told Pilate. "My kingdom is from another place."[10]

When we lived in Rio de Janeiro, Brazil, I learned what it was like to long for home. We loved Brazil. The people were wonderful and the culture warm—but still it wasn't home.

My office was in downtown Rio, only a few blocks from the American embassy. Occasionally I would take my lunch to the embassy and eat. It was like going home for a few minutes. I would walk in the big door and greet the guards in English. I would go into the lobby and pick up an American newspaper. I'd check the box scores or the football standings. I'd chuckle at the cartoons. I even read the want ads. It felt good to think about home.

I would stroll down one of the large corridors and see the portraits of Lincoln, Jefferson, and Washington. Occasionally a worker would have time to chat and I'd get caught up on things back in the States.

The embassy was a bit of the homeland in a foreign country. Life in a distant land is made easier if you can make an occasional visit to home.

Jesus took a long look into the homeland. Long enough to count his friends. "I could ask my Father and he would give me twelve armies of angels." And seeing them up there gave him strength down here.

By the way, his friends are your friends. The Father's loyalty to Jesus is the Father's loyalty to you. When you feel betrayed remember that. When you see the torches and feel the betrayer's kiss, remember his words: "I will never leave you; I will never forget you."[11]

When all of earth turns against you all of heaven turns toward you. To keep your balance in a crooked world, look at the mountains. Think of home.

Chapter 23

Your Choice

"What should I do with Jesus, the one called the Christ?"
Matthew 27:22

*T*he most famous trial in history is about to begin.

The judge is short and patrician with darting eyes and expensive clothes. His graying hair trimmed and face beardless. He is apprehensive, nervous about being thrust into a decision he can't avoid. Two soldiers lead him down the stone stairs of the fortress into the broad courtyard. Shafts of morning sunlight stretch across the stone floor.

As he enters, Syrian soldiers dressed in short togas yank themselves and their spears erect and stare straight ahead. The floor on which they stand is a mosaic of broad, brown, smooth rocks. On the floor are carved the games the soldiers play while awaiting the sentencing of the prisoner.

But in the presence of the procurator, they don't play.

A regal chair is placed on a landing five steps up from the floor. The magistrate ascends and takes his seat. The accused is brought into the room and placed below him. A covey of robed religious leaders follow, walk over to one side of the room, and stand.

Pilate looks at the lone figure.

"Doesn't look like a Christ," he mutters.

Feet swollen and muddy. Hands tan. Knuckles lumpy.

Looks more like a laborer than a teacher. Looks even less like a troublemaker.

One eye is black and swollen shut. The other looks at the floor. Lower lip split and scabbed. Hair blood-matted to forehead. Arms and thighs streaked with crimson.

"Shall we remove the garment?" a soldier asks.

"No. It's not necessary."

It's obvious what the beating has done.

The procurator wouldn't have requested to see this prisoner. Experience has taught him to steer clear of the Jewish squabbles—especially religious ones. But he had to admit he's been curious why this Jesus has stirred the people so.

"They call him a rabble-rouser?" Pilate questions aloud, looking at the guards to his side, giving them permission to chuckle and snap the silence. They do. He shifts in the backless seat and leans against the wall. Were it not for the nature of the charges Pilate would have waved the man and the matter away. But the accusations included words such as *revolt* and *taxes* and *Caesar*. So he is forced to press further.

"Are you the king of the Jews?"

For the first time, Jesus lifts his eyes. He doesn't raise his head, but he lifts his eyes. He peers at the procurator from beneath his brow. Pilate is surprised at the tone in Jesus' voice.

"Those are your words."

Before Pilate can respond, the knot of Jewish leaders mock the accused from the side of the courtroom.

"See, he has no respect."

"He stirs the people!"

"He claims to be king!"

Pilate doesn't hear them. *"Those are your words."* No defense.

No explanation. No panic. The Galilean is looking at the floor again.

Something about this country rabbi appeals to Pilate. He's different from the bleeding hearts who cluster outside. He's not like the leaders with the chest-length beards who one minute boast of a sovereign God and the next beg for lower taxes. His eyes are not the fiery ones of the zealots who are such a pain to the Pax Romana he tries to keep. He's different, this up-country Messiah. As Pilate looks at him the stories begin to come to mind.

"Now, I remember," he says to himself, standing, then stepping down the steps and walking toward a balcony. He stops near the ledge and leans against it. The pigeons stir and a papery rustle of wings is heard as they flutter to the street below.

Pilate reflects on the reports. The strange story of the man over in Bethany. *Dead for, what was it? Three—no, four days. This is the rube they said called him from the grave. And that gathering at Bethsaida. Numbered up to several thousand . . . somebody in Herod's organization told about them. They wanted to make him king. Oh, yes, he fed the crowd.*

Pilate turns and looks at the children playing on the street below. Some are visiting with a guard. *Wanting a handout, no doubt.* The kids don't look good. Frail and thin. Hair stringy. *Lice, probably.* One part of Pilate is troubled because the guard is talking to them and another part is troubled that the guard doesn't help them. All of Pilate is troubled that children such as this have to get sick to begin with. But they do. They do in Rome, they do in Jerusalem.

He looks again at the stooped man who stands in his chambers. *We could use a king,* he sighs. *A king who could make sense out of this mess.*

There was a day when Pilate thought he could. He came to Jerusalem convinced that what was good north of the Mediterranean was good east of it. But that was long ago. That was another Pilate. That was when black was black and white was white. That was when his health was better and his dreams were virgin. That was before the politics. Give a little here to take a little there. Appease. Compromise. Raise taxes. Lower standards. Things were different now.

Rome and noble dreams seem far away. Perhaps that's why he is intrigued by the rabbi. Something in him reminds him of why he came . . . of what he used to be. *They have scourged my back, too, my friend. They have scourged my back, too.*

Pilate looks at the Jewish leaders huddled in the corner across the court. Their insistence angers him. The lashes aren't enough. The mockery inadequate. *Jealous*, he wants to say it to their faces, but doesn't. *Jealous buzzards, the whole obstinate lot of you. Killing your own prophets.*

Pilate wants to let Jesus go. *Just give me a reason,* he thinks, almost aloud. *I'll set you free.*

His thoughts are interrupted by a tap on the shoulder. A messenger leans and whispers. Strange. Pilate's wife has sent word not to get involved in the case. Something about a dream she had.

Pilate walks back to his chair, sits, and stares at Jesus. "Even the gods are on your side?" he states with no explanation.

He has sat in this chair before. It's a curule seat: cobalt blue with thick, ornate legs. The traditional seat of decision. By sitting on it Pilate transforms any room or street into a courtyard. It is from here he renders decisions.

How many times has he sat here? How many stories has he heard? How many pleas has he received? How many wide eyes have stared at him, pleading for mercy, begging for acquittal?

But the eyes of this Nazarene are calm, silent. They don't scream. They don't dart. Pilate searches them for anxiety . . . for anger. He doesn't find it. What he finds makes him shift again.

He's not angry with me. He's not afraid . . . he seems to understand.

Pilate is correct in his observation. Jesus is not afraid. He is not angry. He is not on the verge of panic. For he is not surprised. Jesus knows his hour and the hour has come.

Pilate is correct in his curiosity. Where, if Jesus is a leader, are his followers? What, if he is the Messiah, does he intend to do? Why, if he is a teacher, are the religious leaders so angry at him?

Pilate is also correct in his question. "What should I do with Jesus, the one called the Christ?"[1]

Perhaps you, like Pilate, are curious about this one called Jesus. You, like Pilate, are puzzled by his claims and stirred by his passions. You have heard the stories: God descending the stars, cocooning in flesh, placing a stake of truth in the globe. You, like Pilate, have heard the others speak, now you would like for him to speak.

What do you do with a man who claims to be God, yet hates religion? What do you do with a man who calls himself the Savior, yet condemns systems? What do you do with a man who knows the place and time of his death, yet goes there anyway?

Pilate's question is yours. "What will I do with this man, Jesus?"

You have two choices.

You can reject him. That is an option. You can, as have many, decide that the idea of God becoming a carpenter is too bizarre—and walk away.

Or you can accept him. You can journey with him. You can listen for his voice amidst the hundreds of voices and follow him.

Pilate could have. He heard many voices that day—he could have heard Christ's. Had Pilate chosen to respond to this bruised Messiah, his story would have been different.

Listen to his question: "Are you the king of the Jews?" Had we been there that day we would know the tone of voice Pilate used. Mockery? (You . . . the king?) Curiosity? (Who are you?) Sincerity? (Are you really who you say you are?)

We wonder about his motive. So did Jesus.

"Is that your own question, or did others tell you about me?" [2]

Jesus wants to know why Pilate wants to know. What if Pilate had simply said, "I'm asking for myself. I want to know. I really want to know. Are you the king you claim to be?"

If he had asked, Jesus would have told him. If he had asked, Jesus would have freed him. But Pilate didn't want to know. He just turned on his heel and retorted, "I am not Jewish." Pilate didn't ask so Jesus didn't tell.

Pilate vacillates. He is a puppy hearing two voices. He steps toward one, then stops, and steps toward the other. Four times he tries to free Jesus, and four times he is swayed otherwise. He tries to give the people Barabbas; but they want Jesus. He sends Jesus to the whipping post; they want him sent to Golgotha. He states he finds nothing against this man; they accuse Pilate of violating the law. Pilate, afraid of who Jesus might be, tries one final time to release him; the Jews accuse him of betraying Caesar.

So many voices. The voice of compromise. The voice of expedience. The voice of politics. The voice of conscience.

And the soft, firm voice of Christ. "The only power you have over me is the power given to you by God."[3]

Jesus' voice is distinct. Unique. He doesn't cajole or plead. He just states the case.

Pilate thought he could avoid making a choice. He washed his hands of Jesus. He climbed on the fence and sat down.

But in not making a choice, Pilate made a choice.

Rather than ask for God's grace, he asked for a bowl. Rather than invite Jesus to stay, he sent him away. Rather than hear Christ's voice, he heard the voice of the people.

Legend has it that Pilate's wife became a believer. And legend has it that Pilate's eternal home is a mountain lake where he daily surfaces, still plunging his hands into the water seeking forgiveness. Forever trying to wash away his guilt . . . not for the evil he did, but for the kindness he didn't do.

Chapter 24

The Greatest Miracle

"People walked by . . . and shook their heads, saying, 'You said you could destroy the Temple and build it again in three days. So save yourself! Come down from that cross, if you are really the Son of God!' "
Matthew 27:39-40

*F*unny how taxes and Easter often fall on the same week. They did this year. I began this week with two major tasks: prepare an Easter sermon and pay my taxes.

With apologies to the IRS, one seems very heavenly and the other very earthly. One minute I'm at Calvary, the next at the checkbook. One hour is reverent, the next routine. One reminds me of how God paid it all, and the next reminds me of how I have a lot to pay. (Both the sermon and the tax preparation leave me grateful, however—the first for my Lord, the other for my three little tax deductions.)

I was two days into the week before it hit me. What an appropriate setting in which to study God's sacrifice! For if the cross doesn't make sense on a common week full of common tasks, when does it make sense?

That is the beauty of the cross. It occurred in a normal week involving flesh-and-blood people and a flesh-and-blood Jesus.

Of all the weeks for Jesus to display his powers, his final week would be the one. A few thousand loaves or a few dozen healings would do wonders for his image. Better still, a few Pharisees struck dumb would make life simpler.

Don't just clean the temple, Jesus, pick it up and move it to Jericho. When the religious leaders mutter, make it rain frogs. And as you are describing the end times, split the sky and show everyone what you mean.

This is the week for razzle-dazzle. This is the hour for the incredible. You can silence them all, Jesus.

But he doesn't. Not in Jerusalem. Not in the upper room. Not on the cross.

The week, in many respects, is run-of-the-mill. Yes, it's festive, but its celebrations are due to the Passover, not Jesus. The crowds are large, but not because of the Messiah.

The two miracles Jesus performs aren't intended to draw a crowd. The withered fig tree made a point, but turned few heads. The healed ear in the garden did a favor, but won no friends.

Jesus wasn't displaying his power.

It was an ordinary week.

An ordinary week packed with kids being dressed by impatient moms and dads hustling off to work. A week of dishes being washed and floors being swept.

Nature gave no clue that the week was different than any of the thousands before it or after it. The sun took its habitual route. The clouds puffed through the Judean sky. The grass was green and cattails danced in the wind.

Nature would groan before Sunday. The rocks would tumble before Sunday. The sky would put on a black robe before Sunday. But you wouldn't know that by looking at Monday, Tuesday, Wednesday, or Thursday. The week told no secrets.

The people gave no clue either. For most it was a week of anticipation, a weekend of festivities was arriving. Food to be bought. Houses to be cleaned. Their faces gave no forecast of the extraordinary—for they knew of none.

One would think the disciples would suspect something, but they don't. Corner them and probe their knowledge. They don't know. The only thing they know for sure is that his eyes seem more focused—he seems determined . . . about what they aren't sure.

Tell them that before Friday's dawn they will abandon their only hope, and they won't believe you. Tell them that Thursday night holds betrayal and denial, and they will scoff.

"Not us," they will boast.

For them this week is like any other. The disciples give no clue.

And most importantly, Jesus gives no clue. His water doesn't become wine. His donkey doesn't speak. The dead stay in the graves and those blind on Monday are still blind on Friday.

You'd think the heavens would be opened. You'd think trumpets would be sounding. You'd think angels would be summoning all the people of the world to Jerusalem to witness the event. You'd think that God himself would descend to bless his Son.

But he doesn't. He leaves the extraordinary moment draped in the ordinary. A predictable week. A week of tasks, meals, and crying babies.

A week which may be a lot like yours. Doubtful that anything spectacular has happened in your week. No great news, no horrible news. No earthquakes. No windfalls. Just a typical week of chores and children and checkout stands.

It was for the people of Jerusalem. On the edge of history's most remarkable hour was one of history's unremarkable weeks. God is in their city and most miss him.

Jesus could have used the spectacular to get their attention. Why didn't he? Why didn't he stun them with a loop-a-dee-loop or a double back-flip off the temple? When they demanded, "Crucify him!" why didn't he make their noses grow? Why is the miraculous part of Christ quiet this week? Why doesn't he do something spectacular?

No angelic shield protected his back from the whip. No holy helmet shielded his brow from the thorny crown. God crawled neck deep into the mire of humanity, plunged into the darkest cave of death, and emerged—alive.

Even when he came out, he didn't show off. He just walked out. Mary thought he was a gardner. Thomas had to have hands-on (or hands-in) proof. Jesus still ate, he still talked, he still broke bread with the Emmaus-bound disciples.

Do you see the point?

God calls us in a real world. He doesn't communicate by performing tricks. He doesn't communicate by stacking stars in the heavens or reincarnating grandparents from the grave. He's not going to speak to you through voices in a cornfield or a little fat man in a land called Oz. There is about as much power in the plastic Jesus that's on your dashboard as there is in the Styrofoam dice on your rearview mirror.

It doesn't make a lick of difference if you are an Aquarius or a Capricorn or if you were born the day Kennedy was shot. God's not a trickster. He's not a genie. He's not a magician or a good luck charm or the man upstairs. He is, instead, the creator of the universe who is right here in the thick of our day-to-day world who speaks to you more through cooing babies and hungry bellies than he ever will through horoscopes, zodiac papers, or weeping Madonnas.

If you get some supernatural vision or hear some strange voice in the night, don't get too carried away. It could be God or it could be indigestion, and you don't want to misinterpret one for the other.

Nor do you want to miss the impossible by looking for the incredible. God speaks in our world. We just have to learn to hear him.

Listen for him amidst the ordinary.

Need affirmation of his care? Let the daily sunrise proclaim his loyalty.

Could you use an example of his power? Spend an evening reading how your body works.

Wondering if his Word is reliable? Make a list of the fulfilled prophecies in the Bible and promises in your life.

In the final week those who demanded miracles got none and missed the one. They missed the moment in which a grave for the dead became the throne of a king.

Don't make their mistake.

I still think it ironic that the IRS and the empty tomb are saluted in the same week. Maybe it's appropriate. Don't they say that the only two things certain in life are death and taxes? Knowing God, he may speak through something as common as the second to give you the answer for the first.

Chapter 25

A Prayer of Discovery

"My God, my God, why have you abandoned me?"
Matthew 27:42, TEV

*L*ord?

Yes.

I may be stepping out of line by saying this, but I need to tell you something that's been on my mind.

Go ahead.

I don't like this verse: "My God, my God, why have you abandoned me?" It doesn't sound like you; it doesn't sound like something you would say.

Usually I love it when you speak. I listen when you speak. I imagine the power of your voice, the thunder of your commands, the dynamism in your dictates.

That's what I like to hear.

Remember the creation song you sang into the soundless eternity? Ah, now that's you. That was the act of a God!

And when you ordained the waves to splash and they roared, when you declared that the stars be flung and they flew, when you proclaimed that life be alive and it all began? . . . Or the whisper of breath into the clay-caked Adam? That was you at your best. That's the way I like to hear you. That's the voice I love to hear.

That's why I don't like this verse. Is that really you speaking? Are those words yours? Is that actually your voice? The voice which enflamed a bush, split a sea, and sent fire from heaven?

But this time, your voice is different.

Look at the sentence. There is a "why" at the beginning and a question mark at the end. You don't ask questions.

What happened to the exclamation point? That's your trademark. That's your signature closing. The mark as tall and strong as the words which precede it.

It's at the end of your command to Lazarus: "Come out!"[1]

It's there as you exorcise the demons: "Go!"[2]

It stands as courageously as you do as you walk on the waters and tell the followers: "Have courage!"[3]

Your words deserve an exclamation point. They are the cymbal clash of the finale, the cannon shot of victory, the thunder of the conquering chariots.

Your verbs form canyons and ignite disciples. Speak, God! You are the exclamation point of life itself. . . .

So, why the question mark hovering at the end of your words? Frail. Bent and bowed. Stooped as if weary. Would that you would straighten it. Stretch it. Make it stand tall.

And as long as I'm shooting straight with you—I don't like to see the word *abandon*, either. The source of life . . . abandoned? The giver of love . . . alone? The father of all . . . isolated?

Come on. Surely you don't mean it. Could deity feel abandoned?

Could we change the sentence a bit? Not much. Just the verb.

What would you suggest?

How about *challenge*? "My God, my God, why did you challenge me?" Isn't that better? Now we can applaud. Now we can lift banners for your dedication. Now we can explain it to our children. It makes sense now. You see, that makes you a hero. A hero. History is full of heroes.

And who is a hero but someone who survives a challenge.

Or, if that's not acceptable, I have another one. Why not *afflict*? "My God, my God, why did you afflict me?" Yes, that's it. Now you are a martyr, taking a stand for truth. A patriot, pierced by evil. A noble soldier who took the sword all the way to the hilt; bloody and beaten, but victorious.

Afflicted is much better than *abandoned*. You are a martyr. Right up there with Patrick Henry and Abraham Lincoln.

You are God, Jesus! You couldn't be abandoned. You couldn't be left alone. You couldn't be deserted in your most painful moment.

Abandonment. That is the punishment for a criminal. Abandonment. That is the suffering borne by the most evil. Abandonment. That's for the vile—not for you. Not you, the King of kings. Not you, the Beginning and the End. Not you, the One Unborn. After all, didn't John call you the Lamb of God?

What a name! That's who you are. The spotless, unblemished Lamb of God. I can hear John say the words. I can see him lift his eyes. I can see him smile and point at you and proclaim loud enough for all of Jordan to hear, "Behold, the Lamb of God . . ."

And before he finishes his sentence, all eyes turn to you. Young, tan, robust. Broad shoulders and strong arms.

"Behold the Lamb of God . . ."

Do you like that verse?

I sure do, God. It's one of my favorites. It's you.

What about the second part of it?

What?

The second part of the verse.

Hmmm, let me see if I remember. "Behold the Lamb of God who has come to take away the sins of the world."⁴ Is that it, God?

That's it. Think about what the Lamb of God came to do.

"Who has come to take away the sins of the world." Wait a minute. "To take away the sins . . ." I'd never thought about those words.

I'd read them but never thought about them. I thought you just, I don't know, sent sin away. Banished it. I thought you'd just stood in front of the mountains of our sins and told them to begone. Just like you did to the demons. Just like you did to the hypocrites in the temple.

I just thought you commanded the evil out. I never noticed that you took it out. It never occurred to me that you actually touched it—or worse still that it touched you.

That must have been a horrible moment. I know what it's like to be touched by sin. I know what it's like to smell the stench of that stuff. Remember what I used to be like? Before I knew you, I wallowed in that mire. I didn't just touch sin, I loved it. I drank it. I danced with it. I was in the middle of it.

But why am I telling you? You remember. You were the one who saw me. You were the one who found me. I was lonely. I was afraid. Remember? "Why? Why me? Why has all this hurt happened?"

I know it wasn't much of a question. It wasn't the right question. But it was all I knew to ask. You see, God, I felt so confused. So desolate. Sin will do that to you. Sin leaves you shipwrecked, orphaned, adrift. Sin leaves you aban—

Oh. Oh, my.

My, goodness, God. Is that what happened? You mean sin did the same to you that it did to me?

Oh, I'm sorry. I'm so sorry. I didn't know. I didn't understand. You really were alone, weren't you?

Your question was real, wasn't it, Jesus? You really were afraid. You really were alone. Just like I was. Only, I deserved it. You didn't.

Forgive me, I spoke out of turn.

Chapter 26

The Hidden Tomb

"He put Jesus' body in a new tomb that he had cut out of a wall of rock, and he rolled a very large stone to block the entrance of the tomb."
Matthew 27:60

The road to Calvary was noisy, treacherous, and dangerous. And I wasn't even carrying a cross.

When I had thought of walking Christ's steps to Golgotha, I envisioned myself meditating on Christ's final hours and imagining the final turmoil. I was wrong.

Walking the Via Dolorosa is not a casual stroll in the steps of the Savior. It is, instead, an upstream struggle against a river of shoppers, soldiers, peddlers, and children.

"Watch your wallets," Joe told us.

I already am, I thought.

Joe Shulam is a Messianic Jew, raised in Jerusalem, and held in high regard by both Jew and Gentile. His rabbinic studies qualify him as a scholar. His archaeological training sets him apart as a researcher. But it is his tandem passion for the Messiah and the lost house of Israel which endears him to so many. We weren't with a guide, we were with a zealot.

And when a zealot tells you to guard your wallet, you guard your wallet.

Every few steps a street peddler would step in my path and dangle earrings or scarfs in my face. How can I meditate in this market?

For that is what the Via Dolorosa is. A stretch of road so narrow it bottlenecks body against body. When its sides aren't canyoned by the tall brick walls, they are lined with centuries-old shops selling everything from toys to dresses to turbans to compact discs. One section of the path is a butcher market. The smell turned my stomach and the sheep guts turned my eyes. Shuffling to catch up with Joe, I asked, "Was this street a meat market in the time of Christ?"

"It was," he answered. "To get to the cross he had to pass through a slaughterhouse."

It would be a few minutes before the significance of those words would register.

"Stay close," he yelled over the crowd. "The church is around the corner."

It'll be better at the church, I told myself.

Wrong again.

The Church of the Holy Sepulcher is 1700 years of religion wrapped around a rock. In A.D. 326 Empress Helena, the mother of Constantine the Great, came to Jerusalem in search of the hill on which Christ was crucified. Makarios, Bishop of Jerusalem, took her to a rugged outcropping outside of the northwestern wall of the city. A twenty foot jagged cluster of granite upon which sat a Roman-built temple to Jupiter. Surrounding the hill was a cemetery made up of other walls of rock, dotted with stone-sealed graves.

Helena demolished the pagan temple and built a chapel in its place. Every visitor since has had the same idea.

The result is a hill of sacrifice hidden in ornateness. After entering a tall entrance to the cathedral and climbing a dozen stone steps, I stood at the front of the top of the rock. A glass case covers the tip and the tip is all that is visible. Beneath an altar is a gold-plated hole in which the cross supposedly was lodged. Three crucified icons with elongated faces hang on crosses behind the altar.

Gold lanterns. Madonna statues. Candles and dim lights. I didn't know what to think. I was at once moved because of where I was standing and disturbed by what I was seeing.

I turned, descended the steps, and walked toward the tomb.

The traditional burial spot of Christ is under the same roof as the traditional Golgotha. To see it, you don't have to go outside; you do, however, have to use your imagination.

Two thousand years and a million tourists ago, this was a cemetery. Today it's a cathedral. The domes high above are covered with ornate paintings. I stopped and tried to picture it in its original state. I couldn't.

An elaborate sepulcher marks the traditional spot of Jesus' tomb. Forty-three lamps hang above the portal and a candelabra sits in front of it. It is solid marble, cornered with golden leaves.

An elevated stone path led into the doorway and a black-caped, black-bearded, black-hatted priest stood guard in front of it. His job was to keep the holy place clean. Fifty-plus people were standing in line to enter but he wouldn't let them. I didn't understand the purpose of the delay but I did understand the length of it.

"Twenty minutes. Twenty minutes."

The crowd mumbled. I mumbled. I came as close to the door as I could. The floor was inlaid with still more squares of marble and lanterns hung from the ceiling.

The sum total of the walk began to register with me. Holy road packed with peddlers. The cross hidden under an altar. The entrance to the tomb prohibited by a priest.

I had just muttered something about the temple needing another cleansing when I heard someone call. "No problem, come this way." It was Joe Shulam speaking. What he showed us next I will never forget.

He took us behind the elaborate cupola, through an indiscreet entrance and guided us into a plain room. It was dark. It was musty. It was unkempt and dusty. Obviously not a place designed for tourists.

While our eyes adjusted, he began to speak. "Six or so of these have been found, but are seldom visited." Behind him was a small opening. It was a rock-hewn tomb. Four feet high at the most. The width about the same.

"Wouldn't it be ironic," he smiled as he spoke, "if this was the place? It is dirty. It is uncared for. It is forgotten. The one over there is elaborate and adorned. This one is simple and ignored. Wouldn't it be ironic if this was the place where our Lord was buried?"

I walked over to the opening and stooped like the apostle John did to see in the tomb. And, just like John, I was amazed at what I saw. Not the huge room I'd imagined in my readings, but a small room lit with a timid lamp.

"Go in," Joe urged. I didn't have to be told twice.

Three steps across the rock floor and I was at the other side. The low ceiling forced me to squat and lean against a cold, rough wall. My eyes had to adjust a second time. As they did, I sat in the silence, the first moment of silence that day. It began to occur to me where I was: in a tomb. A tomb which could have held the body of Christ. A tomb which could have encaved the body of God. A tomb which could have witnessed history's greatest moment.

"Five people could be buried here." Joe had entered and was at my side. A couple of my co-travelers were with him. "Two or three would be laid here on the floor. And two would be slid into the holes over here."

"God put himself in a place like this," someone said softly.

He did. God put himself in a dark, tight, claustrophobic room and allowed them to seal it shut. The Light of the World was mummied in cloth and shut in ebony. The Hope of humanity was shut in a tomb.

We didn't dare speak. We couldn't.

The elaborate altars were forgotten. The priest protected sepulcher was a world away. What man had done to decorate what God came to do no longer mattered.

All I could see at that moment, perhaps more than any moment, was how far he had come. More than the God in the burning bush. Beyond the infant wrapped in a feed trough. Past the adolescent Savior in Nazareth. Even surpassing the King of kings nailed to a tree and mounted on a hill was this: God in a tomb.

Nothing is blacker than a grave, as lifeless as a pit, as permanent as the crypt.

But into the crypt he came.

The next time you find yourself entombed in a darkened world of fear, remember that. The next time pain boxes you in a world of horror, remember the tomb. The next time a stone seals your exit to peace, think about the empty, musty tomb outside of Jerusalem.

It's not easy to find. To see it you may have to get beyond the pressures of people demanding your attention. You may have to slip past the golden altars and ornate statues. To see it, you may even have to bypass the chamber near the priest and slip into an anteroom and look for yourself. Sometimes the hardest place to find the tomb is in a cathedral.

But it's there.

And when you see it, bow down, enter quietly, and look closely. For there, on the wall, you may see the charred marks of a divine explosion.

Chapter 27

I Reckons I Will Always Remember That Walk

"In the same way, the Son of Man did not come to be served. He came to serve others and to give his life as a ransom for many people."
Matthew 20:28

*S*o what should I do with Jesus?" Pilate asked it first, but we've all asked it since.

It's a fair question. A necessary question. What do you do with such a man? He called himself God, but wore the clothes of a man. He called himself the Messiah, but never marshaled an army. He was regarded as king, but his only crown was of thorns. People revered him as regal, yet his only robe was stitched with mockery.

Small wonder Pilate was puzzled. How do you explain such a man?

One way is to take a walk. His walk. His final walk. And that is what we have done. We have followed his steps and stood in his shadow. From Jericho to Jerusalem. From the temple to the garden. From the garden to the trial. From Pilate's palace to Golgotha's cross. We have watched him walk—angrily into the temple, wearily into Gethsemane, painfully up the Via Dolorosa. And powerfully out of the vacated tomb.

Hopefully, as you witnessed his walk, you have reflected on your own, for each of us have our own walk to Jerusalem. Our own path through hollow religion. Our own journey down the narrow path of rejection. And each of us, like Pilate, must cast a verdict on Jesus.

Pilate heard the voice of the people and left Jesus to walk the road alone.

Will we?

May I conclude with the stories of three walks, three journeys? The stories of three slaves . . . and the paths they took to freedom.

Mary Barbour could tell you about slavery. First-hand. She remembered the Marse and Marster. She could describe the plantation, the stick-and-mud slave house with the bunks. The long nights. Hot days. Hard whips. Isolation. Mary Barbour could tell you about it. Mary Barbour was a slave.

But she'd rather tell you about freedom. And that is what she did.

In 1935 a worker with the Federal Writers' Project knocked on her door in Raleigh, North Carolina. The Federal Writers' Project was a government-sponsored effort to record the memories of ex-slaves. Over two thousand were interviewed. These, the final voices to speak for the 246 years of bondage in America, did so with earthy eloquence.

They told how they were not allowed to read or write nor purchase or sell merchandise. They couldn't go to church unless invited. Whippings were common. Hard work was a fact of life.

And when freedom came, they weren't ready. They wandered roads looking for work. They were victimized by opportunists. Many ended up back at the same plantation.

But of all the memories, the most vivid, and the one most often shared, was the hour of freedom. The night the Yanks came. The day the Marster told them they could leave. The morning they went up to the "big house" and found it empty.

And of the stories of liberation, none were so specific as Mary Barbour's. She was ten years of age the night her father awoke her and led her to the wagon which would carry them to freedom.

Before you read her words, picture her seated on her porch in Raleigh. It's 1935. Mary Barbour is over eighty years old. She rocks as she thinks. Her tiny body swallowed by the large chair. Her frail fingers tremble as she rubs her nose. Old but eager eyes stare out as if she is gazing into a land far on the horizon. You lean back against the pole and listen to her story.

One of the first things that I remembers was my pappy waking me up in the middle of the night, dressing me in the dark, all the time telling me to keep quiet. One of the twins hollered some, and Pappy put his hand over its mouth to keep it quiet.

After we was dressed, he went outside and peeped around for a minute, then he comed back in and got us. We snook out of the house and along the woods path, Pappy toting one of the twins and holding me by the hand and Mammy carrying the other two.

I reckons I will always remember that walk, with the bushes slapping my legs, the wind sighing in the trees, and the hoot owls and the whippoorwills hollering at each other from the big trees. I was half asleep and scared stiff, but in a little while we pass the plum thicket and there am the mules and the wagon. There am the quilt in the bottom of the wagon, and on this they lays we younguns. And Pappy and Mammy gets on the board across the front and drives off down the road.

I was sleepy, but I was scared too, so as we rides along, I listens to Pappy and Mammy talk. Pappy was telling Mammy about the Yankees coming to their plantation, burning the corncribs, the smokehouses and destroying everything. He says right low that they done took Marster Jordan to the

rip raps down nigh Norfolk, and that he stole the
mules and the wagon and escaped. [1]

Glimmerings of deliverance. Lingerings of the liberation. Six decades later the wind still sighs in the trees and the whippoorwills and hoot owls still holler at each other in Mary Barbour's memory.

The walk to freedom is never forgotten. The path taken from slavery to liberation is always vivid. It's more than a road, it's a release. The shackles are opened and, for perhaps the first time, freedom dawns. "I reckons I will always remember that walk . . ."

Do you remember yours? Where were you the night the door was opened? Do you remember the touch of the Father? Who walked with you the day you were set free? Can you still see the scene? Can you feel the road beneath your feet?

I hope so. I hope that permanently planted in your soul is the moment the Father stirred you in the darkness and led you down the path. It's a memory like no other. For when he sets you free, you are free indeed.

Ex-slaves describe well the hour of deliverance.

Can I tell you mine?

A Bible class in a small West Texas town. I don't know what was more remarkable, that a teacher was trying to teach the book of Romans to a group of ten-year-olds or that I remember what he said.

The classroom was mid-sized, one of a dozen or so in a small church. My desk had carving on it and gum under it. Twenty or so others were in the room, though only four or five were taken.

We all sat at the back, too sophisticated to appear interested. Starched jeans. High-topped tennis shoes. It was summer and the slow-setting sun cast the window in gold.

The teacher was an earnest man. I can still see his flattop, his belly bulging from beneath his coat that he doesn't even try to button. His tie stops midway down his chest. He has a black mole on his forehead, a soft voice, and a kind smile. Though he is hopelessly out of touch with the kids of 1965, he doesn't know it.

His notes are stacked on a podium underneath a heavy black Bible. His back is turned to us and his jacket goes up and down his beltline as he writes on the board. He speaks with genuine passion. He is not a dramatic man, but tonight he is fervent.

God only knows why I heard him that night. His text was Romans chapter six. The blackboard was littered with long words and diagrams. Somewhere in the process of describing how Jesus went into the tomb and came back out, it happened. The jewel of grace was lifted and turned so I could see it from a new angle . . . and it stole my breath.

I didn't see a moral code. I didn't see a church. I didn't see ten commandments or hellish demons. I saw what another ten-year-old—Mary Barbour—saw. I saw my Father enter my dark night, awaken me from my slumber, and gently guide me—no, carry me—to freedom.

"I reckons I will always remember that walk."

I said nothing to my teacher. I said nothing to my friends. I'm not sure I even said anything to God. I didn't know what to say. I didn't know what to do. But for all I didn't know there was one fact of which I was absolutely sure, I wanted to be with him.

I told my father that I was ready to give my life to God. He thought I was too young to make the decision. He asked what I knew. I told him Jesus was in heaven and I wanted to be with him. And for my dad, that was enough.

To this day I wonder if my love has ever been as pure as it was that first hour. I long for the certainty of my adoring faith. Had you told me that Jesus was in hell, I would have agreed to go. Public confession and baptism came as naturally for me as climbing into the wagon did for Mary Barbour.

You see, when your Father comes to deliver you from bondage, you don't ask questions, you obey instructions. You take his hand. You walk the path. You leave bondage behind. And you never, never forget.

Mary Barbour didn't. I haven't. And Tigyne didn't.

Tigyne belonged to the Wallamo tribe in interior Ethiopia. In the years preceding World War II, missionaries carried the message of Christ to this Satan-worshiping tribe. One of the early converts was Tigyne. Raymond Davis was the missionary who knew him . . . and freed him.

Tigyne was a slave. His decision to follow Jesus displeased his master, who refused to allow Tigyne to attend Bible studies or worship. He frequently beat and humiliated Tigyne for his faith. But it was a price this young Christian was willing to pay.

There was another price, however, he could not afford. He couldn't purchase his freedom. For only twelve dollars his master would release him, but for this slave who'd never known a salary, it might as well have been a million.

When the missionaries learned that his freedom could be purchased, they talked it over, pooled some money, and bought his freedom.

Tigyne was now free—both spiritually and physically. He never outlived his gratitude to the men who had redeemed him.

Soon after his day of liberty, the missionaries were expelled from Ethiopia. Twenty-four years passed before Raymond Davis returned to Wallamo. During this quarter of a century Tigyne remained a vivid testimony to the power of freedom. He longed to see Davis again.

When he heard that his friend was coming, he went to the mission station several days in a row to wait. Dates on the calendar or time on the clock had no significance for Tigyne so he came daily to search for Davis.

Finally, Davis arrived, riding in a car driven by a fellow missionary.

When Tigyne saw the vehicle come around the corner, he ran to the window and took Davis's hand and began to kiss it again and again. The driver slowed the car so Tigyne could run beside it. As he ran he yelled to his friends, "Behold! Behold! One of those who redeemed me has returned!"

Finally the car stopped. Davis got out and Tigyne dropped to his knees, put his arms around his friend's legs, and began to kiss his dusty shoes. Davis reached down to bring him to full height and they stood with their arms around each other and wept. [2]

Three ex-slaves. One freed from man, one freed from sin, and one freed from both. Three walks. One destiny—freedom.

It's a walk they will never forget.

"*I reckons I will always remember that walk. . . .*" I pray you never forget your walk or his: Jesus' final walk from Jericho to Jerusalem. For it was this walk that promised you freedom.

His final walk through the temple of Jerusalem. For it was on this walk that he denounced hollow religion.

His final walk to the Mount of Olives. For it was there he promised to return and take you home.

And his final walk from Pilate's palace to Golgotha's cross. Bare, bloody feet struggling up a stony narrow path. But just as vivid as the pain of the beam against his raw back is his vision of you and him walking together.

He could see the hour he would come into your life, into your dark cabin to stir you out of your sleep and guide you to freedom.

But the walk isn't over. The journey isn't complete. There is one more walk that must be made.

"I will come back," he promised. And to prove it he ripped in two the temple curtain and split open the doors of death. He will come back.

He, like the missionary, will come back for his followers. And we, like Tigyne, won't be able to control our joy.

"The one who has redeemed us has returned!" we will cry.

And the journey will end and we will take our seats at his feast . . . forever.

See you at the table.

Study Guide

Chapter 1

Too Little, Too Late, Too Good to Be True

1. *There was a certain honor about being chosen . . . something special about being singled out, even if it was to dig ditches. But just as there was an honor with being chosen, there was a certain shame about being left behind. Again.*

A. Describe a time when you were specially chosen for some occasion. How did it feel? What do you remember most about it? Were you ever passed up for something you really wanted? If so, how did you feel at the time?

B. Read Matthew 20:1-16. Put yourself into the story. How would you feel if you were one of the workers hired at the beginning of the day? If you were hired at the eleventh hour? What point is Jesus trying to make in the landowner's speech of verses 13 through 15? How does verse 16 demonstrate the good news of the gospel?

2. *Get told enough times that only the rotten fruit gets left in the bin, and you begin to believe it. You begin to believe you are "too little, too late."*

A. Have you ever felt like "rotten fruit" or that you were "too little, too late"? What made you feel that way? What do you think Max would say about such assessments of you?

B. Read John 1:43-51. In what way did some people think of Jesus as "rotten fruit" (see verse 46)? How did Jesus react to such an assessment?

C. Read 1 Corinthians 1:26-29. What kinds of people made up the church in Corinth? What might this suggest about the way God sizes up people? According to verse 29, why does God choose to do this?

3. *God has a peculiar passion for the forgotten. Have you noticed?*

A. Have you noticed God's peculiar passion for the forgotten? If so, describe what you have noticed.

B. Read James 1:27 and 2:5. How does God demonstrate his peculiar passion for the forgotten in these two verses? What is to be our response to these people? Why?

C. Read Matthew 11:19. With what kind of people was Jesus known to associate? How does he respond to his opponents' charges? What does this tell you about God's peculiar passion for the forgotten?

4. *Why did he choose you? Why did he choose me? Honestly. Why? What do we have that he needs?*

A. Read Romans 9:10-16. According to Paul, on what basis is God's choice of Isaac made? What did Isaac have that God needed?

B. Read Deuteronomy 7:7-8. What reason does God give in this passage for his love for Israel? Why did he choose her? In what way is God's choice of Israel exactly like his choice of us?

5. *"Shor feels good to be chosen, don't it, boy?" Sure does, Ben. It sure does.*

A. If you have accepted Jesus as your Savior, have you thought much about what it means to be chosen? How does it make you feel?

B. Read Ephesians 1:11-12 and 1 Peter 2:9. What do these passages say about our being chosen by God? What difference does it make to be chosen? How is God's choice of us supposed to change the way we live? Does it change the way you live? Why or why not?

Chapter 2

From Jericho to Jerusalem

1. *Better to go to battle with God's Word in your heart than mighty weapons in your hand.*

A. Read Matthew 20:17-19. In what way does this passage say Jesus was going into battle? In what way was God's Word in his heart? How can you follow his example?

B. Read 1 Samuel 17:45-47. How did David go into battle against Goliath with God's Word in his heart? How does David describe the contest in verse 45? How do we win any of our battles, according to verse 47? How do our daily actions prove that we either believe or disbelieve this verse? What do your daily actions demonstrate?

2. *You can tell a lot about a person by the way he dies.*

A. Why does the way someone dies tell you a lot about him? Have you known anyone whose death told you a lot about him? Read Luke 9:51. How does this verse and Jesus' death tell you a lot about him?

B. Read John 15:13. What does this verse tell you about Jesus' love for you? How does this make you feel?

3. *Forget any suggestion that Jesus was trapped. Erase any theory that Jesus made a miscalculation. Ignore any speculation that the cross was a last-ditch attempt to salvage a dying mission. For if these words tell us anything, they tell us that Jesus died . . . on purpose. No surprise. No hesitation. No faltering.*

A. Read Luke 18:31-34. What did Jesus tell his disciples about what was going to happen? According to verse 31, why did these things have to happen?

B. Read Acts 2:22-23 and 4:27-28. What do these verses tell you about Jesus' death? Although the disciples did not understand Jesus in Luke 18:31-34, did they understand in these passages? If so, what difference did that understanding make to them? What difference would this understanding make to you?

C. Read John 10:14-18. Who are Jesus' sheep in this passage? What does Jesus say He will do for them? What does verse 18 teach you about the crucifixion? How does this passage confirm what Max wrote in the quote above?

Chapter 3

The Sacrificial General

1. *Few will assume responsibilities for the mistakes of others. Still fewer will shoulder the blame for mistakes yet uncommitted. Eisenhower did. As a result, he became a hero. Jesus did. As a result, he's our Savior.*

    A. Think of some leaders you have admired. Did they assume responsibility for the mistakes of others? If so, name some examples. Why is it hard for us to take responsibility for others' mistakes? How is General Eisenhower's action like that of Jesus? How is it different?

    B. Read Matthew 20:25-28. According to Jesus, how do we become great? How do we become first? How did Jesus provide the greatest example of this? How are we to follow his example? Give several practical examples of how you can follow his example this week.

    C. Read Romans 5:6-8. For whom did Christ die? In what way does Jesus' death demonstrate His incomprehensible love for us? How does this passage represent the epitome of Max's principle in this chapter?

2. *Calvary is a hybrid of God's lofty status and his deep devotion. The thunderclap which echoed when God's sovereignty collided with his love. The marriage of heaven's kingship and heaven's compassion. The very instrument of the cross is symbolic, the vertical beam of holiness intersecting with the horizontal bar of love.*

    A. Which is easier for you to think of, God's holiness or his love? Explain your answer. How does the cross symbolize the intersection of these two characteristics?

B. Read Romans 3:25-26 and 11:22. How do these passages confirm Max's quote above? How does the cross satisfy both God's justice and his love?

3. *Jesus didn't write a note, he paid the price. He didn't just assume the blame, he seized the sin. He became the ransom. He is the General who dies in the place of the private, the King who suffers for the peasant, the Master who sacrifices himself for the servant.*

A. In what sense did Jesus become the ransom for us? How was his death far different from anyone else who might die for a friend?

B. Read 2 Corinthians 5:21. How does this verse fit with Max's insight in the quote above? According to this verse, why did Jesus become sin for us?

C. Read Galatians 3:13-14. How did Christ redeem us from the curse of the law? According to verse 14, why did he do this? How does this verse say we take advantage of his work on the cross? Have you taken advantage of it? Explain your answer.

Chapter 4

Ugly Religion

1. *We are wrong when we think God is too busy for little people or too formal for poor protocol. When people are refused access to Christ by those closest to him, the result is empty, hollow religion. Ugly religion.*

A. Have you ever seen ugly religion in practice? If so, what was it like? How were people affected? What impressions did it leave upon you? What, if anything, did you do about it?

B. Read Matthew 20:29-34. Why do you think the crowd rebuked the two blind men? How would you have felt had you been one of the blind men? The answer to Jesus' question seems too obvious—why do you suppose Jesus asked it? What did the blind men do after they were healed? Why do you think they did this?

C. Read Ezekiel 34:1-10. In this passage, Ezekiel uses the term *shepherds* to mean the leaders of God's people. What is wrong with the shepherds in this passage? Do they help people to get to God or do they hinder them? What is God's attitude toward these shepherds? Is it a mild reaction or a strong one? How does this passage reinforce or contradict the above quote from Max?

2. *Something told these two beggars that God is more concerned with the right heart than he is the right clothes or procedure. Somehow they knew that what they lacked in method could be made up for in motive, so they called out at the top of their lungs. And they were heard.*

A. How are we sometimes more concerned with the right clothes or procedure than we are the right heart? Why is it so easy to fall into this trap? How can you avoid falling into it?

B. Read 2 Chronicles 30:18-20. What was the problem in this passage the people faced? What was the solution to the problem? How did God respond to the people in this instance? Why?

C. Read Isaiah 29:13. What is the Lord's complaint in this passage? How can you tell when someone's heart is far from God? How does this passage confirm what Max talked about in the quote?

D. Read Psalm 51:16-17. How is this passage a restatement of Max's quote above? What are the "sacrifices" that God desires of us? In what way is this harder than literal sacrifices? How do you comply with this desire of God's?

3. *Ironic. Of all the people on the road that day, the blind men turned out to be the ones with the clearest vision—even before they could see.*

A. What kind of vision is Max talking about in the quote above? How is your vision?

B. Compare Matthew 16:1-3 with Luke 8:10. How do these passages show that it's possible to have good physical vision but be spiritually blind? How do you improve your spiritual vision?

C. Read 1 Corinthians 1:28-29. How does this passage help explain the quote from Max? What is especially significant about verse 29? How does verse 29 help explain spiritual blindness?

Chapter 5

Don't Just Do Something, Stand There

1. *The Sabbath is the day that God's children in a foreign land squeeze their Father's hand and say, "I don't know where I am. I don't know how I'll get home. But you do and that's enough."*

   A. What does Max mean when he says we are in a foreign land? In what way is the Sabbath a time for getting our bearings? What is to be our focus on the Sabbath?

   B. Read Exodus 20:8-11. What does it mean to *keep* the Sabbath day "holy"? According to verse 11, who *made* it holy? What reason is given for not doing any work on that day? Do you make it a practice to forego work one day out of seven? Why or why not?

   C. Read Psalm 122:1. Why did the psalmist "rejoice" in this verse? How does this verse relate to Max's quote above? Is the psalmist's experience your own? Why or why not?

2. *If Jesus found time in the midst of a racing agenda to stop the rush and sit in the silence, do you think we could, too?*

   A. Why do you think Jesus took time "in the midst of a racing agenda to stop the rush and sit in the silence"? If he needed to do so, why do we so often think we don't need to? What happens when we fail to do so? What happens to you?

   B. Read Luke 4:16. According to this verse, what was it customary for Jesus to do on the Sabbath day? Is this significant for us? If so, how?

3. *Slow down. If God commanded it, you need it. If Jesus modeled*

*it, you need it. God still provides the manna. Trust him. Take a
day to say no to work and yes to worship.*

A. Is it hard for you to slow down? Explain your answer. What
does Max mean when he writes that "God still provides the manna.
Trust him"? Could it be that we don't take a day to say no to work
and yes to worship because we don't trust God for the manna? If so,
how can we change our habits?

B. Read Psalm 92:1-8. Note the title over this Psalm. For what
day was it written? How is this significant? Who is the focus of this
Psalm? How does that focus shape the response of the psalmist?
What is your response to that focus?

C. Read Luke 10:38-42. According to verse 42, what one thing
is needed? Why does Jesus call this better? Note that this must be
chosen; what are you choosing? In what sense can this thing not be
taken away" from those who choose it?

4. *Keep a clear vision of the cross on your horizon and you can
find your way home. Such is the purpose of your day of rest: to
relax your body, but more importantly to restore your vision. A
day in which you get your bearings so you can find your way
home.*

A. Name several ways in which you can keep a clear vision of
the cross on your horizon.

B. Read Hebrews 12:2-3. On what are we to fix our eyes?
According to verse three, what does this accomplish? Conversely, if
we fail to so fix our eyes, what two things always happen? If we
have grown weary or lost heart, could this be the reason?

C. Read Psalm 62:1-2,5-8. Where does David say he finds rest?
Why does he make this so exclusive? In verse 5, whom does David
exhort? Why is this significant? Why does he repeat these lines?
Whom does he exhort in verse 8? What does he exhort them to do?
What reason does he give them for doing so?

D. Evaluate your own experience of the Sabbath day. Are you

regularly taking one day out of seven to rest and focus on God? If
not, why not? If so, how does your experience compare with that of
the writer of Psalm 92? Is there anything you'd like to modify in
your practice of the Sabbath? If so, what?

Chapter 6

Risky Love

1. *The perfume was worth a year's wages. Maybe the only thing of value she had. It wasn't a logical thing to do, but since when has love been led by logic?*

A. Describe your initial reaction to this woman's action. Did you think it foolish? Exorbitant? Profound? Moving? Is love illogical? Or what does Max mean that love is not *led* by logic?

B. Read John 12:1-8. With what character in this episode do you most easily relate? Why? In what ways did Mary take a risk by doing what she did? Try to name some similar ways that we can take such risks today.

C. Read Matthew 26:6-13. In what way was the woman's action a beautiful thing? How was it symbolic of what was to happen? Why do you suppose Jesus said what he did in verse 13?

2. *There is a time for risky love. There is a time for extravagant gestures. There is a time to pour out your affections on one you love. And when the time comes—seize it, don't miss it.*

A. What are the appropriate times for risky love? Describe them. When have you chosen to demonstrate risky love? What was the outcome? Would you do it again? Why?

B. Read Proverbs 3:27-28. What do these verses say about seizing the opportunity to express risky love? If this is an area in which you could improve, how can you do so?

C. Read Philippians 2:25-30. What is the risky love described in this passage? Why was the risk taken? What was the outcome?

In your opinion, was it worth it? Why?

3. *The price of practicality is sometimes higher than extravagance. But the rewards of risky love are always greater than its cost.*

A. In what way does practicality sometimes cost more than extravagance? Do you agree that "the rewards of risky love are always greater than its cost"? Why or why not?

B. Read Luke 6:32-35. List the several instances of risky love that Jesus names in this passage. Why is each one risky? Why does he encourage us to take the risk? What kind of reward are we promised if we take such risks?

4. *Go to the effort. Invest the time. Write the letter. Make the apology. Take the trip. Purchase the gift. Do it. The seized opportunity renders joy. The neglected brings regret.*

A. What opportunities exist for you right now to show risky love? List them. What's stopping you from taking the risk? What do you think of Max's statement that "the seized opportunity renders joy. The neglected brings regret"?

B. Read James 4:17. What does this verse have to do with risky love? How do you respond to it?

Chapter 7

The Guy with the Donkey

1. *Sometimes I like to keep my animals to myself. Sometimes when God wants something I act like I don't know he needs it.*

   A. Can you identify with what Max says in the quote above? If so, in what way? Describe a time when you felt as Max did.

   B. Read Matthew 21:1-7. According to verse 3, how quickly would the owner of the donkey respond to Jesus' request? Why do you think he would respond this way? Is this the normal way you respond? Why or why not?

   C. Compare Matthew 21:3 with Psalm 50:9-12 and Acts 17:24-25. According to these verses, what does God need from us? What do we have that He couldn't do without? In what sense, then, did Jesus need the donkey? In what sense does God need anything from us? Why does this make it such a great privilege to be asked to give him what we have?

2. *All of us have a donkey. You and I each have something in our lives, which, if given back to God, could, like the donkey, move Jesus and his story further down the road.*

   A. Take an inventory of your donkeys. What do you have that could "move Jesus and his story further down the road"? What talents do you have? What resources? What abilities? What gifts?

   B. Read Romans 12:6-8. Note the spirit of the passage. Whatever gifts we have, Paul asks us to use them. Do you recognize any of your gifts among those listed here? Do you know what your gifts are? Are you using your gifts?

C. Read Matthew 25:14-30. With which of the three servants do you most readily identify? Why? How do the first two servants make their master feel? How does the last servant make his master feel? What is the basic lesson Jesus intended to teach with this story?

3. *It could be that God wants to mount your donkey and enter the walls of another city, another nation, another heart. Do you let him? Do you give it? Or do you hesitate?*

A. Why do we sometimes hesitate when we believe God wants to use something we have? What donkey of yours do you think God may want to mount? Describe your thoughts about this.

B. Read 2 Corinthians 9:7. How does this verse relate to giving up your donkey? What does it mean to "decide in [your] heart"? What is wrong with giving reluctantly or under compulsion? What makes God so delighted with a cheerful giver?

4. *God uses tiny seeds to reap great harvests. It is on the back of donkeys he rides—not steeds or chariots—just simple donkeys.*

A. Why do you think God chooses to use the little things to give him glory? Why not big things? Do you ever hesitate giving him little things because they don't seem important or good enough?

B. Read Jeremiah 9:23-24. Why shouldn't wise men boast of their wisdom, strong men boast of their strength, or rich men boast of their riches? How does this passage relate to Max's quote above?

C. Read Judges 7:1-8. Why do you think God whittled down the number of Gideon's troops from 32,000 to 10,000 to 300? What does God's insistence on using little things say to you?

Chapter 8

Hucksters and Hypocrites

1. *Want to anger God? Get in the way of people who want to see him. Want to feel his fury? Exploit people in the name of God. Mark it down. Religious hucksters poke the fire of divine wrath.*

A. Try to think of a few well-known examples where religious hucksters exploited people in the name of God. What did they do? What happened to them? What happened to the people? Describe how you might have seen "the fire of divine wrath" in these instances.

B. Read Matthew 21:12-17. What made Jesus so angry in this incident? What does this tell you about Jesus? Does this have any implications for you? If so, what?

C. Read Titus 1:10-11. How does Paul characterize those who "teach . . . for the sake of dishonest gain"? What do these people do? How are we to respond?

2. *Listen carefully to the television evangelist. Analyze the words of the radio preacher. Note the emphasis of the message. What is the burden? Your salvation or your donation? Monitor what is said. Is money always needed yesterday? Are you promised health if you give and hell if you don't? If so, ignore him.*

A. How carefully do you analyze the religious messages you receive, whether through print, TV, radio, or in person? How can you become better at analyzing these messages? Once you recognize a harmful message, what do you normally do?

B. Read 1 Timothy 6:3-11. In verse 5, how does Paul

characterize those who think that godliness is a means to financial gain? What does he say really is great gain (verse 6)? What is the problem with wanting to get rich (verse 9)? What happens to many who are eager for money (verse 10)? How are we to respond to such practices (verse 11)?

C. Read Romans 16:17-18. What is Paul's exhortation in verse 17? Do you follow his urging? How vigilant are you in this regard?

4. *There are hucksters in God's house. Don't be fooled by their looks. Don't be dazzled by their words. Be careful. Remember why Jesus purged the temple. Those closest to it, may be farthest from it.*

A. Why do you think it's so often true that "those closest to [the temple] may be farthest from it"? When is this a personal problem for you?

B. Read 1 Thessalonians 5:21. What are we commanded to do there? How can you do it?

C. Read Acts 20:28-35. What does Paul urge the Ephesians to do in verse 28? Why does he give this warning (verse 29)? What's the best protection for God's people in this regard (verse 32)? What is one evidence Paul gives of his sincerity (verses 33-34)? How is the saying of Jesus in verse 35 an excellent guide by which to measure someone's teaching?

Chapter 9

Courage to Dream Again

1. *God always rejoices when we dare to dream. In fact, we are much like God when we dream. The Master exults in newness. He delights in stretching the old. He wrote the book on making the impossible happen.*

    A. How practiced are you at dreaming? If it's hard for you, why do you think that is? When you dream, what do you dream about?

    B. Read Isaiah 43:18-19. What sense do you get from this passage about God's delight in new things? Why do you think he has to give us a reminder like this?

    C. Read 2 Corinthians 5:17. Why is it crucial to remember that Christians are *new* creations? What difference does it make?

2. *God can't stomach lukewarm faith. He is angered by a religion that puts on a show but ignores the service—and that is precisely the religion he was facing during his last week.*

    A. Read Matthew 21:18-22. How were Israel's religious leaders like the fig tree in verses 18-19? Was there ever a time when you could have been so characterized? What kind of fig tree are you right now?

    B. Read Luke 18:9-14. Which man in Jesus' story had a lukewarm faith? Which was robust? What did Jesus say about each man? With which man do you most easily identify?

    C. Read Revelation 3:15-16. What is Jesus' reaction to a lukewarm church? Why do you think he is so graphic in this passage? What signs accompany someone who's lukewarm in their faith?

3. *The faith is not in religion, the faith is in God. A hardy, daring*

faith which believes God will do what is right, every time. And that God will do what it takes—whatever it takes—to bring his children home.

A. What is the difference between faith in faith and faith in God?

B. Read Genesis 18:23-25. Note Abraham's question in verse 25. What answer is he expecting? Do you expect the same answer? Based on this question, how do you expect God to act in your life?

C. Read Job 19:25-27. Even though Job is in agony of soul, what is his firm expectation? Who is at the center of his hope? How does that hope transform his outlook?

D. Read 2 Timothy 4:7-8. Describe Paul's great hope as he neared the end of his life. Who is at the center of his hope? Did he expect to be brought home? Is this your expectation as well?

4. *God wants you to fly. He wants you to fly free of yesterday's guilt. He wants you to fly free of today's fears. He wants you to fly free of tomorrow's grave.*

A. Do any of the fears listed in the quote from Max above keep you tightly bound? If so, which ones? What would it take for you to begin to fly free of them?

B. Read Hebrews 2:14-15. According to this verse, why did Jesus take on human form? What kind of freedom did he win for us (verse 15)?

C. Read Matthew 11:28. To what place does this verse instruct us to fly? How can you do this, practically speaking? Are you doing it now? Why or why not?

Chapter 10

Of Calluses and Compassion

1. *No price is too high for a parent to pay to redeem his child. No energy is too great. No effort too demanding. A parent will go to any length to find his or her own. So will God.*

A. If you have children, what price would you be willing to pay to redeem them? What kind of effort would you put out? To what lengths would you go?

B. Read Matthew 18:12-14. What kind of effort is Jesus describing in this story? How does he relate his story to what God actually does (verse 14)?

C. Read 1 John 3:16. How does John define love in this verse? How does it fit with Max's quote above?

2. *God is in the thick of things in your world. He has not taken up residence in a distant galaxy. He has not removed himself from history. He has not chosen to seclude himself on a throne in an incandescent castle. He has drawn near.*

A. Describe your current image of God. Has that image always been the same? If it has changed, describe how it has changed. Was there a time when you felt God was far away? If so, how did your perception change?

B. Read Psalm 139:1-12. How close is God to you right now, according to this passage? How does this make you feel?

C. Read Hebrews 10:19-23. How is it that we can have confidence to draw near to God (verse 19)? In what manner can we draw near to God through Jesus (verse 22)? Why can we "hold unswervingly to the hope we profess" (verse 23)?

3. *God is patient with our mistakes. He is longsuffering with our stumbles. He doesn't get angry at our questions. He doesn't turn away when we struggle. But when we repeatedly reject his message, when we are insensitive to his pleadings, when he changes history itself to get our attention and we still don't listen, he honors our request.*

A. How do we repeatedly reject God's message? In what way are we insensitive to his pleadings? What does Max mean that God honors our request?

B. Read Psalm 103:8-14. What does this passage say about the way God responds to our mistakes? How does verse 14 help explain verse 10? Now read Psalm 130:3-4. If God kept a record of your sins, would you be able to stand? According to this passage, why should we fear God?

C. Read Matthew 21:33-46. Would you describe the landowner in this parable as a patient man? Why or why not? What is the main point Jesus is trying to convey through this story? Why do you think the chief priests and Pharisees understood Jesus was telling this story about them (verse 45)?

4. *God comes to your house, steps up to the door, and knocks. But it's up to you to let him in.*

A. Why do you think God doesn't just knock the door down?

B. Read Ezekiel 33:11. What is God's desire for the wicked as reflected in this verse? Whose job is it to turn from their wicked ways? What is the result of this turning? What happens when they don't turn?

C. Read James 4:8. What does James say is our part in the process he describes? What is God's part? What is the result?

Chapter 11

You're Invited

1. *God is a God who invites. God is a God who calls. God is a God who opens the door and waves his hand pointing pilgrims to a full table. His invitation is not just for a meal, however. It is for life.*

A. Read Matthew 22:1-14. Count how many times a word such as *invite* or *call* is used. What does that tell you about the point of the parable? Who is doing the inviting? Who does he represent?

B. Read Deuteronomy 30:15-16,19-20. What choices did God set before the Israelites? What were the consequences for each? Which choice did he clearly want them to make?

2. *It must sadden the Father when we give him vague responses to his specific invitation to come to him.*

A. How do you think the Father feels when we give him vague responses to his invitation? How would you feel to get such a response? How would you react to such a response?

B. Read Luke 14:16-24. What were the excuses given in this story for not coming to the banquet? Do any of them sound familiar in your own life or acquaintance? What excuses do we make for not accepting God's invitations? How did the master in this story react to those who rejected his invitations? What point was Jesus trying to make?

3. *To know God is to receive his invitation. Not just to hear it, not just to study it, not just to acknowledge it, but to receive it. It is possible to learn much about God's invitation and never respond to it personally.*

A. In what way does receiving God's invitation allow you to know him? What prevents people from responding to God's invitation?

B. Read 2 Timothy 3:7. How does this verse relate to the quote above? Give several examples of the situation described by Paul.

C. Read Matthew 7:24-27 and James 1:22-25. What is the main point of both passages? Why is it so easy to fall into the trap these passages describe? Have you ever fallen into such a trap? If so, how did you get out?

4. *We can choose where we spend eternity. The big choice, God leaves to us. The critical decision is ours. What are you doing with God's invitation?*

A. Answer Max's question: What are you doing with God's invitation?

B. Read Isaiah 55:1-3,6-7. What is God's invitation in this passage? Who is invited? What is the offer? What are the benefits? Have you responded to this invitation?

C. Read Romans 10:9-13. What is the invitation in this passage? How does one accept this invitation? What are the benefits of accepting it? Who may accept the invitation? Have you accepted this invitation?

Chapter 12

Mouth-to-Mouth Manipulation

1. *They hadn't learned the first lesson of leadership. "A man who wants to lead the orchestra must turn his back on the crowd."*

A. What does the maxim quoted above mean to you? Does it make sense? Why or why not?

B. Read Matthew 21:23-27. How does verse 26 illustrate the truth of the maxim quoted above?

C. Read John 12:42-43. What was the main problem of the leaders described in this passage? Did they heed the advice of the maxim quoted above? What was the result of their action?

D. Read 1 Corinthians 11:1. Where is Paul's attention fixed as he writes these words? Is his back to the audience or the orchestra? When you take leadership—whether at home, at work, or in another environment—do you keep this verse in mind? How would it change the way you lead?

2. *God has made it clear that flattery is never to be a tool of the sincere servant. Flattery is nothing more than fancy dishonesty. It wasn't used by Jesus, nor should it be used by his followers.*

A. What is the basic problem with flattery? How do you feel when people use it to try to get from you what they want?

B. Read Matthew 22:15-22. Why is verse 16 an example of pure, unadulterated flattery? How did Jesus respond to it? Why did he use the term *hypocrite* to describe these people?

C. Read Psalm 12:3 and Proverbs 28:23. What is the Lord's opinion of flattery in these passages? Why does God think rebuke is better than flattery?

3. *There are those in the church who find a small territory and become obsessed with it. There are those in God's family who find a controversy and stake their claim to it. Every church has at least one stubborn soul who has mastered a minutiae of the message and made a mission out of it.*

A. Have you ever run into the kind of situation Max describes? If so, explain the situation. What happened?

B. Read Romans 14:19-22. What is the main problem with picking a fight over a disputable issue (verse 20)? What are we to do with our small territories (verse 22)? What is to be our general outlook on such issues (verse 19)?

C. Read 1 Corinthians 1:10-17. How did the Corinthians fall into the trap Max describes in the quote above? What happens when we allow little controversies to divide the body of Christ (verse 17)? How does this happen?

4. *Let go of your territory for a while. Explore some new reefs. Scout some new regions. Much is gained by closing your mouth and opening your eyes.*

A. Is it difficult for you to let go of your territory for a while? If so, why? What can you do to make this easier for you?

B. Read Proverbs 10:19 and James 1:19. What similar advice do Solomon and James give? How are you at following their advice? What can you do to better follow their advice?

C. Read Romans 14:1. How are we instructed to deal with those whom we perceive as being weaker in faith? What are we not to do? Paul assumes in this verse that there will be disputable matters; do we? What kind of issues most often fit this category?

Chapter 13

What Man Dared Not Dream

1. *God did what we wouldn't dare dream. He did what we couldn't imagine. He became a man so we could trust him. He became a sacrifice so we could know him. And he defeated death so we could follow him.*

A. When was the last time God did something in your life that completely surprised you? Describe the incident.

B. Read Matthew 22:41-46. What in Jesus' question so completely startled the Pharisees? Why was the question so hard to answer? Why do you think nobody dared to ask him questions after this incident?

C. Read 1 Corinthians 2:9. What is the point of this verse? To whom are these divine surprises given? Do you qualify for any of these surprises?

2. *Only a God could create a plan this mad. Only a Creator beyond the fence of logic could offer such a gift of love.*

A. Why does Max call God's plan "mad"? Do you agree with him? Why or why not?

B. Read 1 Corinthians 1:18-25. Why does Paul call the preaching of the gospel "foolishness"? What is the main point of this passage (verse 25)? Why does God's plan seem like foolishness to human wisdom?

3. *What man can't do, God does.*

A. Describe any incidents in your life in which what was impossible for you, God did.

B. Read Job 42:2, Jeremiah 32:17, Matthew 19:26, and Luke 1:37. What is the consistent message of all four verses? What confidence does this give you?

4. *When it comes to eternity, forgiveness, purpose, and truth, go to the manger. Kneel with the shepherds. And worship the God who dared to do what man dared not dream.*

A. How is the manger a symbol of eternity, forgiveness, purpose, and truth? Why would kneeling with the shepherds be appropriate?

B. Read Romans 8:3. According to this verse, what did God do that was otherwise impossible? What did he accomplish? How did he do it?

C. Read Ephesians 3:20-21. According to this verse, what is God able to accomplish? How is he able to accomplish it? Where is such power at work? What is the result of these accomplishments? How long does this result last? How does this passage strengthen your confidence in God?

Chapter 14

The Cursor or the Cross?

1. *Computerized religion. No kneeling. No weeping. No gratitude. No emotion. It's great—unless you make a mistake.*

A. Have you ever dabbled in computerized religion? If so, how does it leave you feeling? What did it accomplish? How and why did you abandon it?

B. Read Matthew 23:1-36. Identify each of the "computerized" errors Jesus confronts. Do any of these ever give you problems? Which ones? How do you escape from their grip?

2. *How would you fill in this blank? A person is made right with God through _____.*

A. Fill in the blank as you think appropriate.

B. Read Ephesians 2:8-9. With what is faith contrasted in this verse? What is the problem with works? Why is boasting so terrible?

C. Read Galatians 2:15-16. What is the key element in making a person right with God? How many people will be made right by observing the law? On what are you counting to be made right with God?

3. *Thirty-six verses of fire were summarized with one question: How are you going to escape God's judgment? Good question. Good question for the Pharisees, good question for you and me.*

A. How are we going to escape God's judgment?

B. Read Romans 2:5. What characterizes those who are "storing up wrath for [themselves] for the day of God's wrath"? When will

God's righteous judgment be revealed? How certain is this?

    C. Read Hebrews 2:2-3; 12:25. What is the question in both passages? What is the expected answer?

4. *Why . . . do you think he is known as your personal Savior?*

    A. Is Jesus your personal Savior? How do you know?

    B. Read John 1:12. How does John say Jesus becomes our personal Savior?

    C. Read 1 John 4:14-15. What must we do to be sure that God lives in us?

Chapter 15

Uncluttered Faith

1. *Oh, for the attitude of a five-year-old! That simple uncluttered passion for living that can't wait for tomorrow. A philosophy of life that reads, "Play hard, laugh hard, and leave the worries to your father."*

A. Watch children at play for half an hour. What do you observe? What elements in their play do you wish you could recapture for yourself? What stops you from recapturing them?

B. Read Matthew 18:3-4. In what ways did Jesus insist we become like children? What is the consequence if we don't?

C. Read 2 Corinthians 11:3. What was Paul's concern in this verse? Why should this always be of paramount concern to us?

2. *Complicated religion wasn't made by God. Reading Matthew 23 will convince you of that. It is the crackdown of Christ on midway religion.*

A. What does Max mean by "midway religion"? Why does Christ crack down on it?

B. Read Matthew 23:37-38. What had been Jesus' desire for Jerusalem? How had its people responded? What was the ultimate consequence?

3. *How do you simplify your faith? How do you get rid of the clutter? How do you discover a joy worth waking up to? Simple. Get rid of the middleman.*

A. What does Max mean by the middleman? Who are the middle-men in our culture?

B. Read John 10:10. According to this verse, why did Jesus come to earth? Does this sound complicated? Why or why not? Are you experiencing what Jesus talks about in this verse? Why or why not?

C. Read 1 Timothy 2:5. Who is the one-and-only mediator between God and men? What difference does this make in daily life?

4. *Seek the simple faith. Major in the majors. Focus on the critical. Long for God.*

A. Why do you think we so frequently lose track of the wisdom in Max's quote above? How do we let life and our faith get so complicated? How do you extricate yourself from unnecessary complication?

B. Read Psalm 42:1-2. Is this passage a picture of simple or cluttered faith? Does it sound appealing? Why or why not? Do you know people whose faith mirrors this passage? What do they do that nurtures such a faith?

C. Read Philippians 3:7-9. What was the driving passion of Paul's life, according to this passage? How was this passion energized? Was this a simple passion or a complex one? How does his passion compare to your own?

Chapter 16

Surviving Life

1. *Jesus is honest about the life we are called to lead. There is no guarantee that just because we belong to him we will go unscathed. No promise is found in Scripture that says when you follow the king you are exempt from battle. No, often just the opposite is the case.*

   A. In your own experience, does the above quote ring true? Explain your answer.

   B. Read Matthew 24:1-14. How does verse 6 stand out amidst the list of coming trials? On what is this command based? How does it apply no matter what our situation may be?

   C. Read John 15:18-19 and 16:33. What promise does Jesus make in these two passages? How are we to respond to our lot in life (16:33)? How can we do so (16:33)?

   D. Read 2 Timothy 3:12. What is Paul's expectation in this verse? Who is affected? How do you deal with this promise?

2. *The saved may get close to the edge, they may even stumble and slide. But they will dig their nails into the rock of God and hang on.*

   A. Have you ever been close to the edge? What happened? How did you get pulled back to spiritual safety?

   B. Read Matthew 24:13. Do you see this verse as a promise or a threat? How do you think it's intended?

   C. Read Colossians 1:22-23. In what way is this verse simply an expansion of Matthew 24:13?

3. *The disciples were emboldened with the assurance that the task*

would be completed. Because they had a way to stand in the battle, they were victorious after the battle. They had an edge . . . and so do we.

A. What was the disciples' edge? How is ours exactly the same as theirs?

B. Read Matthew 24:30-31. What encouragement does this passage give to people undergoing trials? How is it an encouragement? Does it encourage you? Why or why not?

C. Read Philippians 1:6. What promise is given in this verse? Is it conditional? How is this promise meant to help you in your walk of faith? Does it?

4. *I could very well be wrong, but I think the command which puts an end to the pains of the earth and initiates the joys of heaven will be two words: "No more."*

A. Why would the statement "No more" be appropriate for initiating the joys of heaven? If you were to guess what those final words would be, what would you guess? Why?

B. Read 1 Thessalonians 4:16-18. In what way is this passage meant to encourage us? What picture comes to mind when you read these verses? Why is it significant the Lord himself will come down from heaven?

C. Read Revelation 19:11-16. What picture do you see here of Christ? Is this an encouraging or a discouraging picture for you? Why?

Chapter 17

Sandcastle Stories

1. *Two builders of two castles. They have much in common. They shape granules into grandeurs. They see nothing and make something. They are diligent and determined. And for both the tide will rise and the end will come.*

A. As you look at your life, what kind of castles do you think you have been building? What attitude have you held about them? If the tide were to come in tomorrow, how would you feel?

B. Read Luke 12:16-21. What kind of castle was the man in the story building? What kind of tide came in? What was the end result? What was Jesus' application?

C. Read Hebrews 9:27. What is the destiny of all of us? What kind of tide is this? Are you ready for this tide?

2. *You've seen people treat this world like it was a permanent home. It's not. You've seen people pour time and energy into life like it will last forever. It won't. You've seen people so proud of what they have done, that they hope they will never have to leave—they will.*

A. In what ways do we sometimes treat this world as if it were a permanent home? How do we act as though life will last forever? How often in a run-of-the-mill day do we stop to realize that one day we'll be leaving this world?

B. Read Matthew 16:26-27. Answer the two questions in verse 26. Are you looking forward to the event described in verse 27, or are you a bit nervous about it? Why?

C. Read James 4:13-14. How would remembering the message of this passage radically change the way we do many things? Why is it that this message seems so easy to forget?

3. *I don't know much, but I do know how to travel. Carry little. Eat light. Take a nap. And get off when you reach the city.*

A. What is the quote above meant to teach us about the way we live our everyday lives?

B. Read Hebrews 11:8-10. How did Abraham practice the wisdom outlined in Max's quote above? What was the key factor in his ability to travel light? In what way is verse 10 as applicable to us as it was to Abraham? Why is it harder in some ways for us to recognize the wisdom of verse 10 than it was for Abraham?

C. Read Hebrews 11:13-16. How could this passage act as a road map for the rest of our lives? How could we be spared a lot of pain if we acted on what it teaches?

4. *Go ahead and build, but build with a child's heart. When the sun sets and the tides take—applaud. Salute the process of life, take your father's hand, and go home.*

A. What does it mean to build with a child's heart? How does the quote above relate to worship?

B. Read Luke 19:11-13. How does the command of verse 13 relate to us? What does Jesus expect us to do until he comes back? What are you doing to comply with this command?

C. Read 1 Corinthians 3:10-15. What is Paul's concern as we continue to build the church (verse 10)? What is the foundation on which we build (verse 11)? What does Paul mean by the various building materials he mentions (verse 12)? What day brings to light how we build (verse 13)? What is the result of our building (verses 14-15)? How is your building going?

Chapter 18

Be Ready

1. *It may surprise you that Jesus made preparedness the theme of his last sermon. It did me. I would have preached on love or family or the importance of church. Jesus didn't. Jesus preached on what many today consider to be old-fashioned. He preached on being ready for heaven and staying out of hell.*

A. Why do you think Jesus made preparedness the theme of his last sermon? What effect does his last sermon have on you?

B. Read Matthew 24:36–25:13. What is the consistent reason given throughout this passage for keeping watch? Are you keeping watch? If so, how? If not, why not?

2. *Jesus doesn't say he may return, or might return, but that he will return.*

A. When you know something is absolutely certain to happen, how do you prepare for it? Are you preparing in the same way for the return of Christ?

B. Read Matthew 16:27; 24:44; Luke 12:40; John 14:3. What do all these verses have in common? When something is repeated several times, what does that usually mean?

3. *Hell is the chosen place of the person who loves self more than God, who loves sin more than his Savior, who loves this world more than God's world. Judgment is that moment when God looks at the rebellious and says, "Your choice will be honored."*

A. Do you often think of hell as a place people choose for themselves? Why or why not?

B. Read 2 Thessalonians 1:5-10. What qualifies the Thessalonians for heaven (verse 10)? Who is punished at the Lord's return (verse 8)? How are these people punished (verse 9)? Which group do you see yourself in?

4. *Our task on earth is singular—to choose our eternal home. You can afford many wrong choices in life. You can choose the wrong career and survive, the wrong city and survive, the wrong house and survive. You can even choose the wrong mate and survive. But there is one choice that must be made correctly and that is your eternal destiny.*

A. Have you made a choice about your eternal destiny? If so, what was that choice? If not, why not?

B. Read John 3:16-18. According to verse 18, what is true of someone who believes in Jesus? What is true of someone who doesn't believe in Jesus? Why did God send his Son into the world (verse 17)? Restate verse 16 in your own words.

C. Read John 20:31. Why did John write his gospel? How do we receive eternal life, according to this verse?

D. Read Acts 17:29-34. What did God overlook in the past (verse 30)? What event is yet future, according to verse 31? What reactions did people have to Paul's message (verses 32-34)? With what group do you most closely identify?

Chapter 19

The People with the Roses

1. *The true nature of a heart is seen in its response to the unattractive. "Tell me whom you love," Houssaye wrote, "and I will tell you who you are."*

   A. What is your response to the unattractive? What do you think of Houssaye's comment?

   B. Read Matthew 25:31-46. What two groups of people are represented here? What happens to each of them? What characterizes each group? Note verse 46: what time frame is mentioned for both groups?

2. *The sign of the saved is their love for the least.*

   A. Do you agree with Max's quote above? Why or why not?

   B. Read Hebrews 13:1-3. What does it mean to keep loving each other as brothers? What is the exhortation of verse 2? How is verse 3 an application of Max's quote above?

   C. Read James 2:1-9. What is the main problem that this passage addresses? What is James's solution? How is verse 8 the heart of this passage?

3. *Jesus lives in the forgotten. He has taken up residence in the ignored. He has made a mansion amidst the ill. If we want to see God we must go among the broken and beaten and there we will see him.*

   A. When was the last time you saw Jesus among the broken and beaten? Describe your experience.

   B. Read Matthew 10:42. What is one sure way to receive a

reward? Is the reward based on great sacrifice? On what is it based?

    C. Read Matthew 11:2-6. What was the question that John the Baptist had for Jesus? How did Jesus answer the question? What significance does this have for Max's quote above?

Chapter 20

Served by the Best

1. *For some, communion is a sleepy hour in which wafers are eaten and juice is drinken and the soul never stirs. It wasn't intended to be as such. It was intended to be an I-can't-believe-it's-me-pinch-me-I'm-dreaming invitation to sit at God's table and be served by the King himself.*

   A. Be honest here—what has been your attitude toward communion? How do Max's words strike you?

   B. Read Matthew 26:17-30. Try to imagine what it would have been like to sit with the Savior at this meal. What are you thinking? What are you feeling? What do you think of Jesus' quote in verse 29?

2. *It is the Lord's table you sit at. It is the Lord's Supper you eat. Just as Jesus prayed for his disciples, Jesus begs God for us. When you are called to the table, it might be an emissary who gives the letter, but it is Jesus who wrote it.*

   A. Who is the emissary Max mentions in the quote above? Why is it significant to remember that it's Jesus who calls you to the table?

   B. Read John 17:20-23. What is the primary request Jesus makes in this passage? How is this especially relevant in talking about the Lord's Supper?

3. *What happens on earth is just a warmup for what will happen in heaven. So the next time the messenger calls you to the table, drop what you are doing and go. Be blessed and be fed and,*

most importantly, be sure you're still eating at his table when he calls us home.

A. What does Max mean when he writes, "Be sure you're still eating at his table when he calls us home"? What should we be careful to do?

B. Read Luke 22:14-18. What word does Jesus use to describe his attitude about eating the Lord's Supper with his disciples? What future event is emphasized in both verse 16 and 18? Do you come to the Lord's table with this emphasis in mind?

C. Read 1 Corinthians 11:26. What does this verse add to your understanding of the Lord's Supper? How is it meant to shape the way we live our Christian lives?

Chapter 21

He Chose You

1. *Jesus knew that before the war was over, he would be taken captive. He knew that before victory would come defeat. He knew that before the throne would come the cup. He knew that before the light of Sunday would come the blackness of Friday. And he is afraid.*

    A. How does it make you feel to realize that Jesus was afraid? Why?

    B. Read Matthew 26:36-46. How does Jesus describe his anguish of soul (verse 38)? What does his posture (verse 39) tell you? In what way were the events described in this passage like a battle?

2. *You need to note that in this final prayer, Jesus prayed for you. You need to underline in red and highlight in yellow his love, "I am also praying for all people who will believe in me because of the teaching." That is you. As Jesus stepped into the garden, you were in his prayers. As Jesus looked into heaven, you were in his vision. As Jesus dreamed of the day when we will be where he is, he saw you there.*

    A. What effect does it have upon you to realize that even as Jesus prepared to go to the cross, he had you in mind?

    B. Read John 17:24. What is Jesus' special request in this verse? Why does he make this request? How does this request make you feel? Why?

3. *It was in the garden that he made his decision. He would rather go to hell for you than go to heaven without you.*

    A. In what way did Jesus go to hell for you? How should this knowledge affect the way we live? Does it? If so, in what way? If not, why not?

    B. Read Ephesians 4:7-10. What light does this passage shed on Max's quote above? What is the significance of the phrase "in order to fill the whole universe"?

    C. Read Hebrews 12:2. According to this verse, why did Jesus endure the cross, scorning its shame? What is important about him sitting down at the right hand of the throne of God?

Chapter 22

When Your World Turns against You

1. *Betrayal is a weapon found only in the hands of one you love. Your enemy has no such tool, for only a friend can betray. Betrayal is mutiny. It's a violation of a trust, an inside job.*

A. Have you ever been betrayed? If so, what hurt the most about your situation?

B. Read Matthew 26:47-56. There are two betrayals described in this passage. Name both of them.

2. *The way to handle a person's behavior is to understand the cause of it. One way to deal with a person's peculiarities is to try to understand why they are peculiar.*

A. What are some ways you can try to understand a person's peculiarities? How can you come to at least partially understand the cause of someone's actions?

B. Read Galatians 6:2. In order to carry one another's burdens, what must you first know? How do you come to know this?

C. Read Philippians 2:19-21. Why did Paul want to send Timothy to the Philippians? What does this assume about Timothy's relationship to the Philippians?

D. Read Hebrews 12:14. What are we here commanded to do? How can we achieve this? Why is it so important to achieve?

3. *As long as you hate your enemy, a jail door is closed and a prisoner is taken. But when you try to understand and release your foe from your hatred, then the prisoner is released and that prisoner is you.*

A. In what way does hatred make you a prisoner? Are you currently its prisoner?

B. Read Matthew 5:43-48. What does Jesus here instruct us to do about our enemies? How can you do this in practice?

C. Read Hebrews 12:15. What does bitterness do to a person? What does it do to others around that person? How are we instructed to deal with bitterness?

4. *To keep your balance in a crooked world, look at the mountains. Think of home.*

A. Read John 18:36. What world was Jesus referring to? What evidence did he offer to show that this earth was not his kingdom?

B. Read Psalm 25:15. What was the psalmist's recipe for staying upright in a crooked world?

C. Read Psalm 73:2-5,13-20. What caused the psalmist some serious attitude problems in verses 2-5? What effect did focusing on this side of life have on him (verses 13-14)? How did he regain his spiritual equilibrium (verses 16-17)? What was his final assessment of the situation (verses 18-20)? In what way does this passage reiterate the message of Max's quote above?

Chapter 23

Your Choice

1. *Jesus is not afraid. He is not angry. He is not on the verge of panic. For he is not surprised. Jesus knows his hour and the hour has come.*

    A. Read John 2:4; 7:6,8,30; 8:20; 13:1. What progression do you see in these verses? In what way do these references make it clear that Jesus was perfectly aware of his mission?

2. *Perhaps you, like Pilate, are curious about this one called Jesus. You, like Pilate, are puzzled by his claims and stirred by his passions. You have heard the stories; God descending the stars, cocooning in flesh, placing a stake of truth in the globe. You, like Pilate, have heard the others speak, now you would like for him to speak.*

    A. Are you curious about Jesus? In what ways? Does he puzzle you? How? Which stories about him are the hardest for you to accept? Why?

    B. Read Luke 22:67-70. What claim does Jesus make for himself in this passage? Why is this the most phenomenal claim of all?

3. *You have two choices. You can reject Jesus. That is an option. You can, as have many, decide that the idea of God becoming a carpenter is too bizarre—and walk away. Or you can accept him. You can journey with him. You can listen for his voice amidst the hundreds of voices and follow him.*

    A. What choice have you made about Jesus? Whose voice are you listening for amidst the hundreds that vie for your attention?

B. Read John 6:60-69. Why did some disciples turn away from following Jesus? Why did Peter continue to follow him? Which decision is most like your own? Why?

4. *Pilate thought he could avoid making a choice. He washed his hands of Jesus. He climbed on the fence and sat down. But in not making a choice, Pilate made a choice.*

A. In what way did Pilate make a choice by not making a choice? How can we make exactly the same mistake?

B. Read Matthew 12:30. In what way does this verse warn against fence sitting?

C. Read John 5:22-29. How does this passage teach that it's impossible to be neutral about Jesus?

Chapter 24

The Greatest Miracle

1. *That is the beauty of the cross. It occurred in a normal week involving flesh-and-blood people and a flesh-and-blood Jesus.*

A. Why is it beautiful that the cross occurred in a normal week involving flesh-and-blood people? What does the normalcy of the week mean to you?

2. *God calls us in a real world. He doesn't communicate by performing tricks. He doesn't communicate by stacking stars in the heavens or reincarnating grandparents from the grave. He's not going to speak to you through voices in a cornfield or a little fat man in a land called Oz. There is about as much power in the plastic Jesus that's on your dashboard as there is the Styrofoam dice on your rearview mirror.*

A. Do you ever long for God to communicate with you through "stacking stars in the heavens" or through "voices in a cornfield"? Explain your answer. What does the Bible's emphasis on *faith* have to do with God's normal methods of communication?

B. Read 2 Corinthians 5:18-20. What did God give to us (verse 18)? To what has he committed us (verse 19)? What title has God given us (verse 20)? What is your part in this commission?

C. Acts 10 tells how an angel told Cornelius to send for Peter so that Peter could explain the gospel to the centurion. Since the angel had no trouble communicating with Cornelius, why do you think the angel himself didn't explain the gospel to Cornelius?

3. *Don't miss the impossible by looking for the incredible. God* *speaks in our world. We just have to learn to hear him. Listen for him amidst the ordinary.*

A. Do you listen for God amidst the ordinary? If so, how? What have you discovered thus far?

B. Read Psalm 19:1-4. In what ways does God continue to speak through the ordinary? How do his messages affect you?

C. Read Acts 17:26-28. What is God's direction of human affairs (verse 26) intended to accomplish (verse 27)? In what sense is God "not far from each one of us"? How does verse 28 relate to Max's quote above?

4. *In the final week those who demanded miracles got none and missed the one. They missed the moment in which a grave for the dead became the throne of a king.*

A. Is it possible for us to be so interested in the miraculous that we miss God? If so, how?

B. Read Matthew 12:39-40. What is wrong with demanding to see a miraculous sign, according to Jesus? What sign did he give the people who demanded a sign? What lesson can we learn from this encounter?

Chapter 25

A Prayer of Discovery

1. *You are God, Jesus! You couldn't be abandoned. You couldn't be left alone. You couldn't be deserted in your most painful moment.*

A. Why is it so hard to accept that Jesus really was abandoned for a time on the cross? Why do you think he was abandoned?

B. Read Matthew 27:45-50: What image comes most clearly to your mind in this scene?

C. Read Psalm 22:1. What impression does it leave upon you that even the words Jesus cried out from the cross were prophesied hundreds of years before they were spoken?

2. *I thought you just sent sin away. Banished it. I thought you'd just stood in front of the mountains of our sins and told them to begone. Just like you did to the demons. Just like you did to the hypocrites in the temple. I just thought you commanded the evil out. I never noticed that you took it out. It never occurred to me that you actually touched it—or worse still that it touched you.*

A. Why was it not possible for God simply to send sin away? Why did it have to be *taken* out?

B. Read 2 Corinthians 5:21. What did God do to him who had no sin? Who is the one who had no sin? For whom did he do this? Why did he do this? What is your reaction to this?

C. Read Galatians 3:13-14. Who redeemed us from the curse of the law? How did he do this? Why did he do this?

3. *Your question was real, wasn't it, Jesus? You really were afraid. You really were alone. Just like I was. Only, I deserved it. You didn't.*

A. In what way did we deserve to be alone? Why did Jesus not deserve to be alone? Why did God reverse our roles?

B. Read Isaiah 53:4-5. How many instances of this role reversal can you spot in this passage? With what main impression does this passage leave you?

C. Read 1 Peter 3:18. For what did Christ die? What role reversal is described here? What was the purpose of this reversal? Have you personally appropriated what this verse describes?

Chapter 26

The Hidden Tomb

1. *Shuffling to catch up with Joe, I asked, "Was this street a meat market in the time of Christ?" "It was," he answered. "To get to the cross he had to pass through a slaughterhouse."*

A. What is especially poignant about the observation in the quote above?

B. Read Matthew 27:26-31. In your opinion, what was the cruelest torture inflicted on Jesus? Why do you think God allowed all of this to happen?

C. Read 1 Corinthians 5:7. What was a Passover lamb (see Exodus 12:1-13)? In what sense was Christ our Passover lamb?

2. *"Wouldn't it be ironic," he smiled as he spoke, "if this was the place? It is dirty. It is uncared for. It is forgotten. The one over there is elaborate and adorned. This one simple and ignored. Wouldn't it be ironic if this was the place where our Lord was buried?"*

A. What would be ironic about the state of affairs outlined above? Why would it be ironic?

B. Read Matthew 27:57-61. What details are given about the tomb? Why do you think more details are not given?

C. Compare Isaiah 52:14, Isaiah 53:2 and Luke 2:7. What do all of these verses have in common? Taken together, what do they say about God's need to do things in a flashy way? Why do you think he operates this way?

3. *God put himself in a dark, tight, claustrophobic room and allowed them to seal it shut. The Light of the World was mummied in cloth and shut in ebony. The Hope of humanity was shut in a tomb.*

   A. How does the quote above make you feel? Why?

   B. Read Matthew 12:40. Did Jesus expect to die? Did he expect to be buried? What attitude did he seem to take toward it in this verse?

   C. Read 1 Corinthians 15:3-4. Why does Paul say that the information he conveys in this passage is "of first importance"? What crucial items does he name? Why are they all crucial?

4. *When you enter the tomb, bow down, enter quietly, and look closely. For there, on the wall, you may see the charred marks of a divine explosion.*

   A. In what way could the empty tomb be considered a better symbol of the Christian faith than the cross? Which symbol better conveys God's power? Why?

   B. Read Acts 2:22-24. According to verse 24, what was impossible? Why was this impossible?

   C. Read 1 Corinthians 6:14. What attribute of God is stressed in this verse? What did it accomplish? What will it accomplish?

Chapter 27

I Reckons I'll Always Remember That Walk

1. *What do you do with such a man? He called himself God, but wore the clothes of a man. He called himself the Messiah, but never marshaled an army. He was regarded as king, but his only crown was of thorns. People revered him as regal, yet his only robe was stitched with mockery.*

   A. Answer the question above: What do you do with such a man?

   B. Read Matthew 28:1-10. Why do you think the angel sat on the stone in verse 2? Why did he speak to the women but not the guards? How is it that the women could be both afraid and filled with joy at the same time (verse 8)?

2. *Where were you the night the door was opened? Do you remember the touch of the Father? Who walked with you the day you were set free? Can you still see the scene? Can you feel the road beneath your feet?*

   A. Try to answer Max's questions above. Describe the scene if you can.

   B. Read Acts 26:12-18. List the elements Paul uses in his testimony. Does the way he gives his testimony give you any ideas about the way you could give yours? Explain your answer.

3. *I told my father that I was ready to give my life to God. He thought I was too young to make the decision. He asked what I knew. I told him Jesus was in heaven and I wanted to be with him. And for my dad, that was enough.*

A. How can you tell when someone is ready to give his life to God?

B. Read Romans 10:9. How do you give your life to God, according to this verse?

C. Read 2 Corinthians 6:1-2. According to this passage, when is it appropriate to give your life to God?

4. *The journey isn't complete. There is one more walk that must be made. "I will come back," he promised. And to prove it he ripped in two the temple curtain and split open the doors of death. He will come back. He, like the missionary, will come back for his followers. And we, like Tigyne, won't be able to control our joy. "The one who has redeemed us has returned!" we will cry. And the journey will end and we will take our seats at his feast . . . forever. See you at the table.*

A. Are you looking forward to the day described in the quote above? If so, how does this expectation shape the way you live now? Do you expect to be at the table? If so, how? If not, why not?

B. Compare 1 Thessalonians 3:12-13 and 5:23-24. How does Paul connect the expectation of Christ's coming with our conduct right now? What supplies the power for godly living (5:24)?

C. Think back over the insights in this book. If you had to name one that was most meaningful to you, what would it be? Will your life be different from interacting with this insight? How?

D. Take time to pause and thank God for sending his Son to earth to die in your place. Thank him for his love. Thank him for his patience. Thank him for his provision. Spend some uninterrupted time simply basking in the gracious presence of the One who does all things well.

Notes

A Word Before

1. I've limited this book to the events in Christ's final week as recorded by Matthew.

Chapter 1, Too Little, Too Late, Too Good to Be True

1. Corinthians 1:26.

Chapter 2, From Jericho to Jerusalem

1. Mark 10:32.
2. James Michener, *Texas* (New York, N.Y.: Random House, 1985), 367.
3. Matthew 20:18-19.
4. Acts 2:23.
5. Jeremiah 29:11.
6. Romans 8:1.
7. Hosea 11:9b.
8. Ephesians 3:18-19.

Chapter 3, The Sacrificial General

1. "D-Day Recalling Military Gamble that Shaped History," *Time*, 28 May 1984, 16.
2. Matthew 20:28.
3. Daniel 7:4.
4. Daniel 7:5.

Notes

5. Daniel 7:6.

6. Daniel 7:7.

7. Daniel 7:13-14.

8. For further reference consider the Book of Enoch, an intertestamental book completed sometime around 70 B.C. This ancient manuscript tells us what picture came to the minds of people when they heard the title "the Son of Man."

Note these phrases excerpted from the Book of Enoch.

And this Son of Man whom thou hast seen shall put down the kings from their thrones,
And shall loosen the reins of the strong
And break the teeth of sinners.
And he shall put down the kings from their thrones and kingdoms because they do not extol and praise him . . . (Enoch 46).

When they see that Son of Man
Sitting on the throne of his glory.
And the kings and the mighty and all who possess the earth shall bless and glorify and extol him who rules over all, who was hidden.
. . . all the elect shall stand before him on that day.
And all the kings and the mighty and the exalted and those who rule the earth
Shall fall before him on their faces,
And worship and set their hope on the Son of Man,
And petition him and supplicate for mercy at their hands.
. . . he will deliver them to the angels for punishment,
to execute vengeance on them because they have oppressed his children and his elect (Enoch 62).

For that Son of Man has appeared,
And has seated himself on the throne of his glory,
And all evil shall pass away before his face,
And the word of that Son of Man shall go forth
And be strong before the Lord of Spirits (Enoch 69).

9. Matthew 19:28.

10. Matthew 24:30; Mark 13:26; Luke 17:26,30.

11. Matthew 26:64.

12. Mark 9:31.

13. Mark 9:32.

14. Matthew 20:28 isn't the only passage which speaks of the dualism of God. He is the Lord "who shows mercy, who is kind . . . but he does not forget to punish guilty people" (Exodus 34:6,7). He is the only "good God." At the same time he is the "Savior" (Isaiah 45:21). He is equally "full of grace and truth" (John 1:14). He is the God who in wrath can remember mercy (Hebrews 3:2). In a precious insight Micah states to God, "You will not stay angry forever, because you enjoy being kind" (Micah 7:18). "God," states Paul, "is kind but also very strict" (Romans 11:22). He is able to "judge rightly and . . . make right any person who has faith in Jesus" (Romans 3:26).

We find it difficult to hold simultaneously in our minds a God who is the Judge who punishes and the Lover who forgives. But that is the God of Scripture. He is the God who "in a marvelous and divine way loved us even when he hated us." (John R. W. Stott, *The Cross of Christ* [Downers Grove, Ill.: InterVarsity Press, 1986], 131.) He is, at the same time, angry at our sin and touched by our plight.

Chapter 4, Ugly Religion

1. Matthew 20:29-30.
2. Matthew 20:34.
3. "Wilford Hall turf fight puts patients at risk," *San Antonio Light*, 3 February 1990, A1, A16.
4. 2 Chronicles 30:18-20.
5. 2 Chronicles 30:20.
6. Jeremiah 29:13.

Chapter 5, Don't Just Do Something, Stand There

1. Luke 4:16, emphasis added.
2. Psalm 39:6, NIV.

Chapter 6, Risky Love

1. Matthew 26:10. Matthew waits until chapter 26 to tell a story which chronologically should appear in chapter 20. By referring to John's Gospel we see the anointing by Mary in Bethany occurred on Saturday night (John 12:1). Why does Matthew wait until so late to record the story? It appears that he sometimes elevates theme over chronology. The last week of Christ's life is a week of bad news. Chapter 26 and 27 sing the woeful chorus of betrayal. First the leaders, then Judas, then the apostles, Peter, Pilate, and eventually all the people turn against Jesus. Perhaps with the desire to tell one good story of faith in the midst of so many ones of betrayal, Matthew waits until Matthew 26 to tell of Simon and Mary.
2. Matthew 26:13.

Chapter 7, The Guy with the Donkey

1. Matthew 21:2-3.
2. Matthew 5:41-42.

Chapter 8, Hucksters and Hypocrites

1. *Paul Harvey's For What It's Worth*, ed. Paul Harvey, Jr. (New York, N.Y.: Bantam Books, 1991), 118.
2. Mark 11:11.
3. Matthew 21:12-13.
4. Titus 1:11.
5. Romans 16:17-18.
6. Mel White, *Deceived*, as quoted by John MacArthur, Jr. in *The MacArthur New Testament Commentary, Matthew 1-7* (Chicago, Ill.: Moody Press, 1985), 462.

Notes

Chapter 9, Courage to Dream Again

1. It is obvious by comparing Matthew with Mark that the incident occurred on two days. Part on Monday and part on Tuesday. The cleansing of the temple occurred between these two parts.

Why the difference in the two accounts? Matthew chooses to describe the incident topically while Mark describes it chronologically. Mark states that Jesus cursed the tree on Monday morning (11:12-14) then cleansed the temple (11:15-19). The second part of the fig tree story—the amazement of the disciples (11:20-24)—happened on Tuesday morning as the disciples and Jesus were returning to Jerusalem.

Matthew is topical in his teaching. He groups the two events, but in doing so, doesn't contradict Mark. He wants to tell the entire story with no interruptions. He begins by saying, "Now, in the morning . . ." (21:18). He doesn't say the next morning. And when he begins to report on the disciples amazement, he simply says, "And when the disciples saw it . . ." (21:20).

By combining Matthew and Mark we see that the cursing of the tree took place on Monday and the commentary occurred on Tuesday. There is no conflict. One writer is topical and the other chronological. Each has it advantages. (*See* William Hendricksen, *The Gospel of Matthew* [Grand Rapids, Mich.: Baker Book House, 1973], 773).

2. Matthew 21:21.
3. Revelation 3:15-16.
4. Matthew 21:22.

Chapter 10, Of Calluses and Compassion

1. Matthew 21:33-45.
2. Matthew 22:1-14.
3. Deuteronomy 4:32-34.
4. Hosea 11:8-9.
5. Romans 8:16.
6. 2 Samuel 7:19.
7. 2 Samuel 7:15.
8. Matthew 21:43.
9. Acts 13:46.
10. Matthew 12:24.
11. Deuteronomy 4:35.
12. Romans 2:4.
13. Revelation 3:20, KJV.

Chapter 11, You're Invited

1. Isaiah 1:18.
2. Isaiah 55:1.
3. Matthew 11:28.
4. Matthew 22:4.

5. Mark 1:17.
6. John 7:37.
7. Matthew 21:28-32.
8. Matthew 22:1-14.
9. Revelation 3:20.
10. Hebrews 9:27, RSV.

Chapter 12, Mouth-to-Mouth Manipulation

1. Matthew 21:23.
2. Matthew 21:26.
3. Matthew 22:15-17.
4. Psalm 12:3, NIV.
5. Proverbs 28:23, NIV.
6. Paul Aurandt, *Paul Harvey's the Rest of the Story* (New York, N.Y.: Bantam Books, 1977), 123.
7. Dennis Tice, "Did Adam and Eve Have Navels?" Unpublished work. Used by permission.

Chapter 13, What Man Dared not Dream

1. Matthew 22:42.

Chapter 14, The Cursor or the Cross?

1. Matthew 23:5.
2. Matthew 23:5.
3. Matthew 23:6.
4. Matthew 23:7.
5. Matthew 23:5.
6. Matthew 23:13-24.
7. Matthew 23:33.
8. Romans 3:28.

Chapter 15, Uncluttered Faith

1. Matthew 18:2-3, Phillips.
2. Matthew 23:8-12.
3. Matthew 23:8.
4. Matthew 23:9.
5. Matthew 23:10.

Chapter 16, Surviving Life

1. Matthew 24:1-2.
2. William Barclay, The Gospel of Matthew, Vol. 2, *Daily Study Bible Revised Edition*, (Philadelphia, Penn.: The Westminister Press, 1975), 305.
3. The imperfect tense is used, implying a continual, unending course of action.

4. Matthew 24:2, author's paraphrase.
5. Matthew 23:38.
6. Barclay, 307.
7. John 16:33.
8. Matthew 24:5.
9. Matthew 24:6.
10. Matthew 24:7-8.
11. Matthew 24:9.
12. *The Wall Street Journal,* 15 January 1992, A-P1.
13. Matthew 24:13.
14. Matthew 24:14.
15. Acts 2:5.
16. Matthew 24:14.

Chapter 17, Sandcastle Stories

1. Matthew 24:36.
2. Matthew 25:1-13.
3. Matthew 25:14-30.
4. Matthew 25:31-46.

Chapter 18, Be Ready

1. Matthew 24:45-51.
2. Matthew 25:1-13.
3. Matthew 25:14-30.
4. Matthew 24:42.
5. Matthew 25:31.
6. Matthew 24:44.
7. Acts 1:11, NIV.
8. Hebrews 9:28.
9. I Thessalonians 5:2, NIV.
10. Matthew 25:32-33.
11. Matthew 25:41.
12. 1 Thessalonians 5:9, NEB.
13. Hebrews 9:27.
14. Matthew 7:24-27.
15. Matthew 7:13-14.
16. Paul Lee Tan, *Encyclopedia of 7007 Illustrations* (Rockville, M.D.: Assurance Publishers, 1979), 1086.

Chapter 19, The People with the Roses

1. "Promises to Keep," *Focus on the Family Magazine,* June 1989, 21-22.
2. Matthew 25:35-36.
3. Hebrews 11:6b.
4. Matthew 25:40. I like Martin Luther's commentary on this verse. " 'Here

below, here below,' says Christ, 'You find me in the poor: I am too high for you in heaven, you are trying to climb up there for nothing.' Thus it would be a very good idea if this high command of love were written with golden letters on all the foreheads of the poor so that we could see and grasp how near Christ is to us on this planet." S. D. Bruner, *Matthew, V. II, The Churchbook* (Dallas, Tex.: Word Publishing, 1991), 923.

5. *San Antonio Express-News,* 3 April 1991, 2.

Chapter 20, Served by the Best

1. Matthew 26:18.
2. John 13:5.
3. A sacrament is a gift from the Lord to his people.
4. A sacrifice is a gift of the people to the Lord.
5. There are sacrificial moments during the Supper. We offer up prayers, confessions, and thanksgivings as sacrifice. But they are sacrifices of thanksgiving for a salvation received, not sacrifices of service for a salvation desired. We don't say, "Look at what I've done." We instead, in awe, watch God and worship what he has done.

Both Luther and Calvin had strong convictions regarding the proper view of the Lord's Supper.

"Out of the sacrament and testament of God, which ought to be a good gift received, they (the religious leaders) have made up for themselves a good deed performed." (Martin Luther, *Luther's Works American Edition,* 36:49.)

"He (Jesus) bids the disciples to take: He himself, therefore is the only one who offers. When the priests pretend that they offer Christ in the Supper, they are starting from quite another source. What a wonderful case of topsy-turvy, that a mortal man to receive the body of Christ should snatch to himself the role of offering it." (John Calvin, *A Harmony of the Gospels,* 1:133.)

(As quoted by Frederick Dale Bruner in *Matthew V. 2, The Churchbook* [Dallas, Tex.: Word, Inc., 1991],958).

6. Romans 8:34.
7. Luke 12:37.

Chapter 21, He Chose You

1. John 17:20-21.

Chapter 22, When Your World Turns against You

1. Matthew 26:46.
2. Matthew 26:56.
3. Matthew 26:59.
4. Matthew 26:50.
5. Matthew 26:15.
6. Matthew 26: 48-49.
7. Matthew 26:49.

8. James 1:2.
9. Matthew 26:64.
10. John 18:36.
11. Hebrews 13:5.

Chapter 23, Your Choice

1. Matthew 27:22.
2. John 18:34.
3. John 19:11.

Chapter 25, A Prayer of Discovery

1. John 11:43.
2. Matthew 8:32.
3. Matthew 14:27.
4. John 1:29.

Chapter 27, I Reckons I Will Always Remember That Walk

1. *My Folks Don't Want Me to Talk About Slavery,* ed. Belinda Hurmence (Winston-Salem, N.C.: John F. Blair Publishing, 1984), 14-15.
2. Raymond Davis, *Fire On the Mountain* (publisher information unavailable).

Max Lucado speaks weekly at the Oak Hills Church of Christ in San Antonio, Texas. If you would like to order tapes of his messages, you can request a tape catalogue from:

UpWords Tapes
8308 Fredericksburg Road
San Antonio, Texas 78229